MW01705483

The Inside
Letters From Alaska
To The Outside

Bill Hauser

Publication Consultants Since 1978

PO Box 221974 Anchorage, Alaska 99522-1974
books@publicationconsultants.com—www.publicationconsultants.com

ISBN 978-1-59433-104-6
Library of Congress Catalog Card Number: 2009930224

—First Edition—

Manufactured in the United States of America.

Acknowledgements

Oh, my. There are so many people to thank for their involvement in my project. This book. It would not have been possible without the many people who participated in so many activities and adventures that allowed me to learn and write about Alaska during the past 29 years. This begins with my family who were involved in many of the activities that were the nuclei of many experiences and thoughts that became the chapters of this book.

First; I say thank you to my wife, Karel, who has been a frequent companion in a myriad of Alaska adventures. She has offered continuous support, suggestions, patience, and encouragement and especially, typing services. Next, thanks to Bill, Donna, and, Peter, our son, daughter, and son-in-law, respectively, who were also part of many activities and contributed ideas, proofreading, and critiques to fuel my writings.

There were many other people who were involved with events and activities discussed in this book; most often, Hazzy, Joe, Loren, and Nick, but there were many work colleagues, relatives and friends who gave me the opportunities to see and experience Alaska and to share it with them and you.

Over the many years of writing and sharing these letters, various readers offered feedback and suggestions that led to this publication. I thank them for their encouragement.

Thanks go to Marthy Johnson for her editing and encouragement.

Evan Swensen provided constant support and suggestions in the process of the publication.

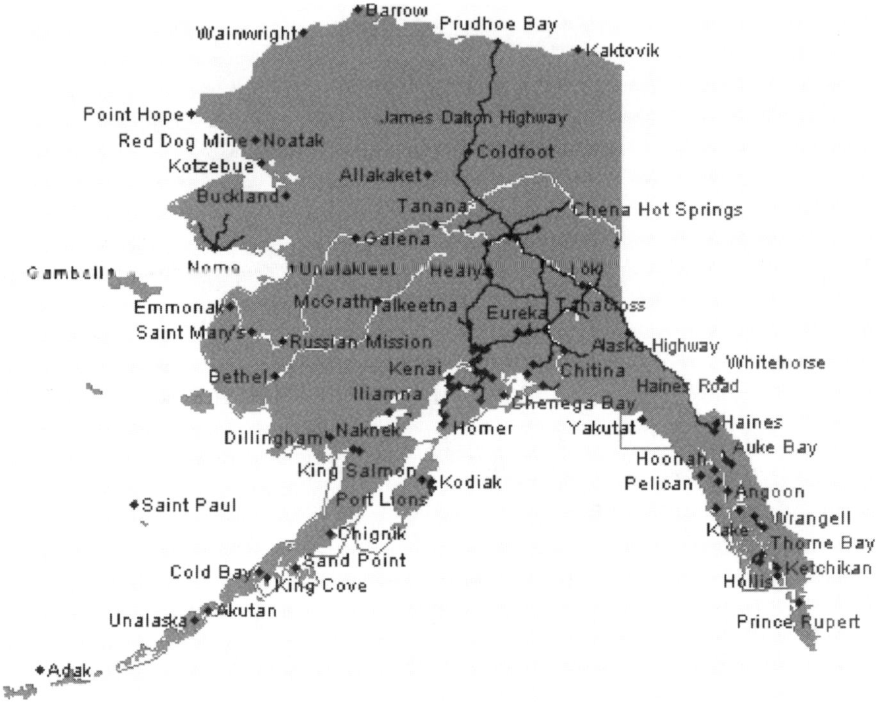

Map of the State of Alaska with locations of cities and largest villages. Black lines indicate the primary roads and white lines indicate the Yukon and Kuskokwim Rivers.

Contents

Introduction

Short stories about living, working, and recreating in Alaska

Winter, 2008.

Hey, Hello.

How are you doing? It is a pleasant time here in Anchorage, Alaska. It is snowing today, but it is a very pretty and gentle snow and the redpolls and chickadees are already busy doing their job at our feeders. We are happy for the snow because cross-country ski races are going on and it is just a week from the start of our annual winter carnival, the Fur Rendezvous, which includes the famous World Championship sprint sled dog races as well as snow sculptures, fireworks, a parade, and many other events and activities. In a week, the long distance Iditarod sled dog race from Anchorage to Nome will start.

When I moved here with my wife, Karel, son, Bill, and daughter, Donna, in 1980, some folks laughed and reminded us that Los Anchorage is not really Alaska—but you can see it from there. Nevertheless, we have enjoyed living here and I appreciate the amenities of a big city while I have been fortunate to make frequent visits to the *real* Alaska through both work and recreational activities. But getting around in Alaska is a lot different and a lot less predictable than getting around in Anchorage. Alaska, you see, is a big piece of landscape with an area roughly equal to a third of the Lower 48—as the rest of the United States is called. Also, places outside Alaska are referred to simply as Outside.

Our road system, however, is limited and vast spaces of the state are accessible only by small charter aircraft or watercraft during much of the year. Winter overland travel is enhanced by the use of snowmachines. Travelers may make travel plans and schedule trips, but the actual schedule is simply defined by weather conditions. When conditions are not safe, travelers must wait, and late arrivals simply explain, "I was weathered in." This is an explanation all Alaskans instantly recognize and understand and no further discussion is required.

Recreating and working in Alaska, therefore, often includes long periods of waiting and indeterminate lengths of time with nothing to do. Experienced travelers plan ahead and have a paperback book handy to read and pass the time. Most often, I have typically used that time to write, usually, in the form of a letter to share my feelings and experiences with relatives and friends, many of whom live in the Lower 48. So, that is just what this book is all about: letters and experiences from inside Alaska to the Outside.

These letters represent a sort of verbal snapshot of what was going through my mind and of the experience that I was living. As such, they were not preplanned, but represent a flow of thoughts. As I gathered them into book form, they have not been extensively rewritten or recreated, but lightly edited only to improve readability.

I am feeling good and I hope that you are having a good day, too.

Talk with you later.

Bill Hauser

Section One—Live Alaska

Chapter One
Bear Watching

Bear watching has become an important tourist activity in Alaska and Katmai National Park has become a popular destination to safely observe and photograph concentrations of coastal brown bears at close range.

July 14, 1996

Hello, good evening.

It is hard to start this letter. It is just hard to know *how* to start.

Donna just said, "This was a good day." She is right. Presently, she is unfolding her sleeping bag and complaining about a big lump right under where her butt is supposed to be. We have moved into the last of the 20 available campsites here at Katmai National Park and Preserve. We will be here for nearly a week. We are here to photograph bears. And do some fishing, too. And camp. (Can you believe this, Donna has started doing sit-ups!)

We arrived at about 4:30 p.m. and began to set up camp and make supper. Before we could even eat supper, we had already seen 10 bears. After supper, we went to the lower viewing platform and saw perhaps 20 more. As well as a large-sized bull moose. So far, it has been absolutely awesome--and it has just begun. We have five more days to go. I am tired.

More later.

July 18

That was not much of a start. I will try harder this time.

Bears. We came here to see bears. We see bears everywhere! Anywhere. Any time. Middle-sized bears. Miniature bears. Singles. Doubles, more. The most we saw all at the same time was *13*. And a mother bear with two cubs; another with three cubs. They are close and far and, thankfully, none has been too close.

Bill Jr., Donna, and I had flown from Anchorage to King Salmon, where we boarded a floatplane to get here to Katmai National Park and Brooks Lodge.

The trip actually began last January, when after two hours of nonstop dial and redial, I made a phone-in reservation to camp here for the week. It has been a wonderful trip so far. When we get tired of doing whatever we are doing, we go look for another bear. We have rarely waited longer than a half hour before another one showed up.

Brooks River is part of the headwaters of the Naknek drainage in Bristol Bay and most of the streams and rivers of Bristol Bay are crowded with sockeye, or red, salmon. Brooks River has an abrupt 6-to 8-foot falls, which is a challenge for the salmon to jump. They pause below the falls until they are ready to jump. While they wait, they become bear food. These bears migrate

A grizzly or, brown, bear follows the shore of Naknek Lake beside the Katmai National Park campground. Note the distinctive shoulder hump and dished-in brow that distinguish a grizzly from a black bear.

from 40 or 50 miles to take advantage of this tremendous food source; and because the food is abundant and easy to catch, they become unusually tolerant of other bears at nearby feeding stations.

Brooks Falls is a good place to see the feeding bears and watch their interactions–the fighting and posturing and the scuffles that happen. The National Park Service has built a viewing platform that provides a safe vantage point. A mile or so downstream, at the mouth of the river, another viewing platform allows great viewing of bears and lake scenery. But of course, we see bears everywhere, like along the shoreline of the lake, which is just near the campground. Beautiful. A couple of times actually in the campground. Eating a meal can be a challenge if a bear comes ambling along the shore. Drop everything and grab a camera! Although we have seen many more bears than I expected and we have more pictures than I want to pay for, each sighting is different and special and offers a more unique picture than the last. Even if it is mealtime–when a bear shows up, take a picture.

Donna especially enjoys seeing the cubs. They frolic and tumble along behind mama. She catches a fish and holds it for them. They growl and tussle and try to sound ferocious. The big bears, however, do not need to *try*. When they growl and tussle, they *are* ferocious. After you've seen a fight and watched

A short hike leads to the summit of Dumpling Mountain and a panoramic view of Naknek Lake, Brooks River and Brooks Lake.

bears running by within 20 feet, it can be very spooky walking back through the woods, especially under low-light conditions. Trust me.

We have been so busy watching bears and taking pictures of bears that aside from a trip to the Valley of Ten Thousand Smokes, we have hardly had time to fish. Tomorrow, always tomorrow.

Oh, I almost forgot–Brooks Lodge, a commercial venture on a park inholding, provides an extra dimension to our visit. Today, we had an all-you-can-eat noon meal which we took full advantage of. And 2 days ago, we took showers for $4 each. Interesting place. And, Brooks Lodge rents cabins for visitors if you don't want to camp out.

The Valley of 10,000 Smokes was covered by 700 feet of ash by the eruption of Mount Novarupta in June, 1912.

July 20

We must leave today. I am lying in my sleeping bag nearly ready to awaken Donna and Bill so we can have breakfast and begin to pack. Did I mention that Karel opted not to come along on the trip? She thoroughly enjoys camping, but she does not enjoy camping while bears are playing just outside her tent. I think that only once, maybe twice, was a bear actually sighted within

The upstream viewing platform overlooks Brooks River Falls which slows the upstream migration of sockeye salmon. The concentration of salmon causes a concentration of feeding grizzly bears.

Visitors are restricted to designated trails and the viewing platforms but bears can go wherever they want. This viewing platform overlooks the lower end of Brooks River and the floating bridge, which crosses the river near the river outlet.

the confines of the campground. But we often see them at the edge of the lake, about 100 yards from the campground.

The most important rule here at Brooks Camp—or anyplace where bears are common—is to practice good behavior. The Park Service strictly enforces this rule. No food in a tent or in a pack. Always make noise to avoid surprising a bear. Bears always have the right of way. Where does a brown bear sleep? Anywhere it wants to. And, let sleeping bears lie. If they happen to take a nap on the trail to a viewing platform, nobody can use the trail until the bear gets up and leaves. Always be alert.

Bill Jr.'s comments:

It has been an amazing experience for me. To live here in Alaska for 16 years and then come here to see this makes me realize how much more there is in Alaska outside Anchorage. The landscape is pretty much the same as what I

Females with cubs avoid the larger concentrations of feeding bears and are always alert for both fish and other bears.

am used to seeing; only it is more pristine and clean. Actually, the weather is not clear, but that is southwestern Alaska. This is a secluded real wilderness that is marred by an overabundance of tourists. *Many* Europeans, many Lower 48-ers, and some Alaskans, too. So far, the Californians have taken the prize for the most surprising tourists.

Watching these bears has been a wonderful experience in such a beautiful place. It is only after you leave Alaska that you grasp the magnitude of its beauty and majesty in comparison with the rest of the United States. There has been no better way to practice the rules of bear safety than to fish and live around them. It has been great seeing a real wilderness in its natural beauty in this 7-day stay.

Donna writes:

As the preceding pages have said, this was a wonderful experience. It was so much more than anything I had expected. I thought that Katmai would be interesting, but that I would quickly get sick of it. That didn't exactly happen. As Bill once said, it was like we were on our own safari.

Bears were everywhere. It was amazing that we could get so close to the bears. They were very tolerant. They tolerated people in their house and they tolerated each other. They were often closer than 50 feet.

One mother bear even used people to her advantage. At the falls, where mostly large males fed, she would stash her cubs right up under the platform so she could go fish for them. This close proximity to humans helped to protect the cubs from the boars. Of course, I did not mind. Seeing the cubs was my favorite part. They were cute.

Just one more extreme of Alaska, that is, one more beautiful extreme of Alaska. It was a great privilege to experience the thriving communities of beautiful but intimidating bear in a gorgeous setting.

From all of us:

We always like to see wildlife when we are out, but watching bears for a week at Katmai is a truly awesome experience.

Love.

Bill, Donna, Bill

June 20, 2008

Oh, wait, there is more … Brooks Lake and Brooks River are part of the headwaters of Bristol Bay, the world's largest sockeye salmon production factory. Brooks River drains into Naknek Lake and the Naknek River which, together with seven other major river systems, flow into Bristol Bay. All 5 species of North American Pacific salmon are found in Bristol Bay; however, sockeye, or red salmon are by far the most numerous. Why would this be? Simple. Habitat. More specifically, the drainages of Bristol Bay contain abundant amounts of habitat that is well suited to the rearing requirements of young sockeye salmon.

As the adult sockeye salmon migrate through the shallow waters of the Bristol Bay estuary, they are harvested by commercial fishermen. The Bristol Bay salmon fishery has been carefully managed and it is recognized as an example of a successful, stable fishery that has maintained a long-term sustainable harvest. In fact, this fishery is the largest sockeye salmon fishery in the world.

Sockeye salmon have the most complex life history of all the Pacific salmon. After sockeye salmon enter freshwater to lay their eggs, they swim upstream until they encounter a lake where they pause in their migration several weeks or a month before they move on to the spawning grounds, where they excavate nests or redds. Most spawning is in midsummer in small streams and rivers, but also, to a lesser extent, along the margins of some lakes and islands.

The eggs are buried in redds where they incubate until about midwinter. After hatching, the embryonic fry, called alevins, remain in the gravel until they absorb their yolk sac, when they emerge from the gravel to become free swimming. Typically, newly emerged fry migrate to lakes where they rear. Fry that emerge from redds downstream from lakes are genetically programmed to swim upstream toward the lake, whereas those from redds upstream from lakes migrate downstream to the lake. The rearing fry prey mainly on microscopic free-swimming invertebrate animals called plankton. Sockeye salmon rear in lakes from 1 to 3 years before they migrate to the ocean as smolts.

Sockeye salmon migrate for one to three years around the North Pacific Ocean, where they feed mainly on small shrimp-like organisms. They grow and mature until they return to freshwater to spawn and die.

After they die, the nutrients that have been stored in their bodies are released from the carcasses. The nutrients are dissolved in the water and fertilize the very base of the food chain that provides food for the young salmon after they hatch and migrate from the spawning areas into the many lakes of the region where they rear. The freshwater habitats of the eight river and lake systems and the fertile ocean currents are the machinery of the factory that converts the raw material into a valuable commercial harvest and more spawning adults to maintain the cycle. Thus, the salmon themselves provide the raw material to drive the Bristol Bay sockeye salmon factory production.

One last tidbit. Each population of sockeye salmon is somehow uniquely adapted for their particular stream and lake system and, collectively, they compose the huge, biologically complex grouping of populations that make up the entire Bristol Bay sockeye salmon resource.

Link: Brooks Lodge in Katmai National Park:
http://www.katmailand.com/lodging/brooks.html

Chapter Two

Urban Moose

We are used to seeing moose in Anchorage,
but this year exceeded all expectations.

September 29, 2007

Hi all.

Hey, I just have to tell you about the truly awesome week—even for Alaska—that I have had.

A week ago, I sent this e-mail.

Subject: Good day moose hunting

Hey, hi.

I must tell you of my good fortune just this morning. I started at daylight when it was almost too dark to shoot and I was home by 10:30 a.m. I was in east Anchorage. I saw at least 15, perhaps as many as 20 moose. There were at least three bulls. One was trophy class. It had five cows and it chased off a smaller bull. I got up close, within about 20 yards, to a different medium-sized but very respectable bull. I got off about eight shots. It was a good morning, but I was shooting print film so I won't know the results till the film is processed.

Most were farther off but I just walked up on the medium-sized bull that was just off the edge of the trail. It did a lot of grunting and peeing. Finally it lay down and all I could see was an antler. Everything pretty much settled down by about 9 a.m. Later, I learned that this bull stood up about 10 minutes after I left when some people with dogs came by and other photographers got some good shots (of the moose). The rut is clearly underway but I think that it has not yet peaked so some good shooting may still be available.

For Anchorageites, I was on the Powerline Pass trail beside Flattop Mountain.

Bill

That was a good day. Wow, it was amazing to see so many moose in one place in such a short amount of time. There was one group of five cows with one big bull. There were singles and other small groups. And, there was some mixing and matching. Most were several hundred yards away, across a small valley. Bulls were following cows and chasing other bulls.

It was a wonderful fall morning although it was a small disappointment to find that the high tundra was past its peak of colors and was mostly an off-brown. When the tundra is at its peak and brightened by sunshine, the reds of the dwarf dogwood and yellows of the low-growing willows lay out a spectacular backdrop. This day, the upper edges were trimmed with a dusting of fresh, bright, early snow which, in turn, was highlighted by a brilliant deep blue sky. And, there seemed to be moose everywhere.

When moose gather in Chugach State Park for the rut, it is not unusual to find close-up views of trophy-class bulls.

I had heard that this time and location offered a good opportunity to watch large numbers of moose exhibiting rutting behavior and I was not greatly surprised to see this many animals. The actual experience, however, was so much more impressive than I had expected. Karel and I are always on the lookout to see wildlife whether we are around home or on the road; and on occasion, we will make a special effort just to see wildlife such as waterfowl, deer, Dall sheep, or marine mammals. Nevertheless, we had never taken advantage of this small effort for such a big reward.

This fall has been more wet and gloomy than usual, but I have kept an eye on the weather forecast. A few days later, when it looked like we would have a break in the weather, I was ready to revisit the area. Karel and my friend Joe went along. We have all lived in Anchorage for more than 25 years so we have seen plenty of moose and other wildlife, but we were still awed by what we saw.

We parked in the lot, but before we started on a trail, we saw a small bull moose at a distance of about 100 yards. We walked 150 yards to a viewing platform and saw another. Moments later, we saw the small bull again; this time at a distance of about 20 yards. I think that Karel and Joe thought we had done well for a morning, but as we edged back, near the parking lot, we saw another moose. A bigger bull. Trophy class. It was walking on one of two parallel access trails that we wanted to take to Powerline Pass Trail. We took the other trail.

Powerline Pass Trail is perched about halfway up on the south side of a long valley that runs east and west and it affords a panoramic view of the opposite, south-facing hillside. We arrived before the sun had pushed its way over the far ridge, so the broad, open, tundra-filled meadow was in deep shadow, but almost immediately we began to pick out large dark shapes that were slowly moving about. There! A big bull! It was surrounded by five cows. Another bull. More cows. We strolled east on the trail. There! Right beside the trail. Three. No, four moose. At about 100 yards. Across the valley; another group of four. And, there! What? "Oh, look, there is a photographer." Then, another. These folks had crossed the valley on a spur trail and were up close and personal with the big bull and the cows. Eventually, there were two more. They must have had a field day. Several groups of mountain trail runners also wound their way down the mountain. Once, they had to detour around the moose that seemed to be oblivious to the people and focused on the matter at hand.

We watched the show and took pictures for about two hours. We saw as many as about twenty moose. Certainly, we had multiple sightings both within and between trips, but that thought did not diminish our awe.

Back at the access trail, two hikers breathlessly reported that they had just seen a "huge bull, just right back there and right beside the trail." Soon, we were clicking off more shots at another nice bull, at close as about 50 feet. It was another great day of moose hunting and it was only a little after 10 a.m. But there is more.

The next morning, I drove to the other edge of town for some late-season fishing in Campbell Point Lake in Kincaid Park. As I slowed to a stop in the small parking lot, I discovered a mature bald eagle sitting not 50 feet away at the edge of the lake. It was nervous and flew off, but stopped at the top of a nearby spruce. I grabbed my camera and walked to the fishing float and did some shooting of the eagle and the lake which reflected the bright glowing fall colors. I turned and walked back, but before I reached my car, a cow moose and calf walked across the parking lot, within about 30 feet.

They posed at lakeside and worked their way around the north edge of the lake as I clicked away. As I geared up and put on my waders, I realized that fish were quite active near the shore, so I decided to try my luck from shore before I launched my float tube. I made several casts. I may have even caught a fish. A movement off to my right emerged into the form of a moose! A respectable, medium-sized bull. It walked with its nose nearly touching the ground along the same trajectory that the cow and calf had followed less than 20 minutes earlier. This moose, too, stepped to the edge of the lake and took a long drink as it posed for me in the midst of a reflection of a wall of golden leaves.

I returned to my fishing with frequent gazes back over my shoulder. I made my way back onto the fishing float where the fish cooperated and soon got me more focused. I began to catch 7-inch-long salmon that had been raised at the hatchery and released here for the benefit of winter ice fishers. They only wanted to chase a small black fly that I retrieved just under the water surface in 6-inch strips. It would have been boring to catch so many small fish so easily but they hit the fly during the pause so hooking them was the challenging part. It was great practice for setting the hook with a strip strike. We have all been taught to set the hook by quickly raising the rod tip. That works okay, but if the fish is missed, the fly will be pulled well away from the fish. A strip set works with a quick tug of the line by the left hand. The fly moves only as far as the length of the tug and stays in the view of the fish. This hook-setting technique is widely used in saltwater fly fishing. On one cast, I had three hits and misses before I hooked a fish on the fourth set. Great fun.

All of the above happened in just six days.

But, two days later, I looked out our living room window and spotted a Wilson's snipe probing the soggy turf with its long bill for insects or worms. Again, I got out my camera and set up the long lens and tripod. I took a number of shots and went away. Some time later, I looked again and was surprised that the snipe had moved only about a foot. The light was better, so I shot several more frames. As I watched, the bird suddenly flinched and hunkered down. A magpie sailed by, about 15 feet above the ground. Now, the snipe was on full alert and I got ready to shoot again. Just as I tripped the shutter, there was a commotion and a white flash of wings. The magpie had circled around and pounced on the snipe. Both flew off and it was over.

Wow. All that wildlife in just eight days. Only in Alaska. No, not even Alaska. I had not even left Anchorage.

I had just parked the car when this moose cow and calf walked across the parking lot. A few minutes later, this bull followed their route across the parking lot, down to the water, and around the lake.

October 14, I wrote in an e-mail:

Hello.

I had something interesting happen today and I thought you may find it cute.

As I walked back to the house, this morning, after a short workout, I turned the last corner and spotted a moose cow and calf in our side yard just chowing down on our pathetic mountain ash. This mountain ash is pathetic looking because it gets chowed on by moose at least monthly throughout the year. Moose love mountain ash. We are lucky this one has survived as well as it has.

It is that time of year when we should be wrapping the mountain ash and the birches and the shrubs in chicken wire to prevent this sort of thing. Last Saturday, we were off doing other things and Sunday it was raining.

Here in Alaska, we always enjoy seeing moose even in the neighborhoods, but we like to enjoy our trees and shrubbery, too, so we take NIMBY—Not In My Back Yard—quite seriously when it comes to moose and trees. And, of course, we know moose can be dangerous around traffic and under certain conditions. Cows with young calves can be especially dangerous, but by this time of year, they usually respond to hazing by simply standing their ground and staring back with a seemingly bland non response. Eventually, they usually just amble off casually with apparent disdain.

So, this morning, I did what needed to be done. I brazenly approached the pair, and from about 50 feet, I shished loudly and waved, then snapped my towel. I got the usual response. I continued my noisemaking and as I approached closer, her shoulder hackles began to rise. No surprise. But, then, she took a step or two toward me and the hackles rose even more and she began to drool. She was a very large cow. One of the biggest cow moose that I have seen. By now, I was at about 25 feet. The calf responded with several quick steps toward the back of the house. The cow was distracted and turned. Hackles were stiffly up.

Now their attention became focused on a shrub in the backyard. Good. I turned and went around the other side of the house past the side of the main entrance. I surprised them again as I came around the corner of the house making a loud fuss. She was about 20 feet away. This time, there was nothing bland in her response. In fact, she was quite emphatic. Hackles were really up! Like I have never seen before! She was on full alert. And she did not hesitate. She immediately closed to half the distance!

Suddenly, I realized that she was not playing this game according to the usual rules. I knew that if I ran, she would easily run me down. And then, I realized something else.

The front door was still locked!

I had trouble getting the key out of my pocket. "Take off your gloves, dummy!" I did not panic, but my fingers just did not want to work right! Finally, I saw that she had turned. I got the door open and got in.

The cow and calf went off between the houses and across the street as if I had never bothered them. At least they were NIMBY.

October 19, I wrote in another e-mail:

Wow. What month this has been. A monthful of moose. I have seen more moose in the last month than ever and they were closer and more dramatic than ever, too.

Late this morning, I was in the upstairs bedroom when I glanced out of the window to check the bird feeder. Chickadees and nuthatches were there getting fueled up. Then, as my gaze expanded past our lot line, I was startled to see a good-sized cow moose with two big calves approaching our yard where they settled in to do some refueling of their own. One calf was a small bull with thick nubbins that resembled fur-covered golf balls. They started eating almost everything they found. Overhanging branches from our neighbor's mountain ash, some bushes. Red currants and raspberries. Sniffed and passed on mums. Strawberries. Freeze-dried green peas and a dead tomato bush. Pansies. The cow even ate the dried rhubarb leaves and stem. I called to Karel and she looked out from the downstairs window.

When I raised my view, again, I saw the bull. It was walking purposefully across the greenbelt directly toward our house. Before long, we had four moose in our backyard.

This bull was fully mature and large of body and antlers. It grunted with a series of unhh, unhh, unhh. It reached its head down and nibbled on fallen mountain ash leaves and eventually got down on its front knees so it would not need to stretch so far. Finally, it lay down to chew its cud right in the back corner of our lot. The cow seemed to ignore the bull, but made a sort of moaning sound. The calves wandered back and forth and ate whatever they encountered.

Karel had a ringside seat as one moose walked within 10 feet of her window.

Soon, the cow disappeared from view around the south side of our house and really hurt our mountain ash even though Karel and I had just covered it two days ago with chicken wire. The calves followed right behind. The bull obviously was intent on the cow and he would not let her move far away. As he rounded the corner of the house, she bolted. She would not let him get close.

The cow slipped and nearly fell as she dashed across the street. Now, the cow and calves began chowing down on a small tree on one side of our neighbor's yard while the bull munched on the tree by their driveway. The grunting and moaning continued. The neighbors flashed away with their cameras. When the bull crossed the driveway, the cow, with the calves, bolted again, between the neighbors' houses. And over the chain link fences. The bull dutifully followed. Other neighbors were shooting pictures now. Then it was over.

You know, I felt kind of sorry for that bull. He barely had time to eat or chew his cud.

Keep in touch.

Love from Alaska

Bill

It's not unusual to see moose in a neighborhood in Anchorage but it is unusual to see four at the same time. This bull pursued the cow across the greenbelt, through our yard, across the street, past our neighbor's house, and over a chain link fence. The cow would not allow the bull to approach within 100 feet.

April 7, 2008

Oh, wait, there is more … The tag line for the Municipality of Anchorage is *Big Wild Life* and, in fact, that line is quite descriptive. Anchorage probably has the largest and most diverse population of urban wildlife of any city of similar size. The summer population of moose in Anchorage is approximately 200 to 300, with as many as 1,000 during the winter. Some say that it is easier to see a moose in Anchorage than in Denali National Park. But there is much more. Bears are regularly sighted within the city; approximately 250 black bears and sixty grizzly bears live in the area. Approximately 30 wolves live in the Anchorage area and lynx are sometimes seen. Dall sheep are often seen from the highway just south of the city. Beluga whales are resident to the waters of upper Cook Inlet and beavers are busy cutting down trees along local streams. Eagles are not uncommon and, periodically, great horned owls will strike a person on the head in a defensive move or by mistaking a moving head of hair for a rabbit.

This of course, is a mixed blessing. We always enjoy seeing wildlife, but moose and vehicles do not mix well and over 100 moose per year are killed in Anchorage by cars. There is vehicular damage, of course, and sometimes there are human fatalities from the encounter, too. Two people were stomped to death by moose in the early 1990s and serious encounters happen regularly. Cow moose are especially dangerous in late spring when they are very defensive of their young calves. The extensive Anchorage trail system is typically within greenbelts or park areas and moose like to travel on these multi-use trails, too. Periodically, bull moose get their antlers tangled up in strings of holiday lights, swing sets, and clothes lines and sometimes they need to be tranquilized to become disentangled.

Moose are browsers and they are especially fond of birch trees and decorative trees such as mountain ash. They prune red currant, but usually leave red raspberry alone. Tulips are particularly vulnerable because they are some of the earliest greens available. Fortunately, they avoid daffodils.

Bears and wolves are seen much less often than moose. Grizzly bears are more secretive than black bears and they gravitate toward salmon spawning areas in a heavily wooded park on the east side of the city. Back-country hikers and runners must be prepared for possible bear encounters. Black bears love to raid garbage cans and when they become habituated, they can become quite bothersome and potentially dangerous. The bear usually becomes euthanized and the homeowner may be fined for improperly stored thrash. Wolves are rarely seen, but several dogs were killed or hurt by wolves in 2007, some while on walks with their owners.

There are several good wildlife viewing areas in the city. Kincaid Park and the Tony Knowles Coastal Trail are good places to look for moose. Beluga whales may be spotted from the Port of Anchorage, Point Woronzof, and stops along the Seward Highway southeast of the city.

Excellent opportunities exist for bird watching in the Anchorage Coastal Wildlife Refuge and Potter Marsh. Together these compose a huge wetland that attracts more than 220 species of resident or migrant birds, including bald eagles, trumpeter swans, Canada geese and snow geese, ducks, and arctic terns. Potter Marsh is especially accessible and it includes a boardwalk with interpretive displays.

One last tidbit ... If you really want to see Alaska wildlife and you have limited time, the Alaska Zoo is in Anchorage and the Wildlife Conservation Center is located at Portage on the Seward Highway.

The Anchorage Convention and Visitors Bureau web site has all sorts of information about the municipality, including wildlife.
Link: http://www.anchorage.net/index.html

Chapter Three
Growing Pains

Children and parents grow in different ways.

February 7, 1998

Hello.

It has been a while since I have written, but I think about our friends and relatives and I like to tell them about things we have been up to lately.

Today, I guess that I feel a need to tell you about a special revelation that has come into my life and I am compelled to share it with you. I have come abruptly to that stage in a father's life when he must realize that his little girl is really not a little girl any longer and that she does not need his help much more. What an awful situation! This reminds me of a lesson I learned several years ago with Bill Jr. A parents' responsibility is to spend about 18 or so years helping their child, and hold their hand and provide guidance and advice and caring and worrying, until suddenly the responsibility changes without warning. The parents must quietly and abruptly reverse all they have worked for and, instead, help their children to go away. To make them leave. To send them and to push them off into the world on their own and without the helping hands that deep down inside you know they cannot survive without.

Donna has done well in high school and is working hard to find just the right university. She has been accepted at the University of Washington and at Western Washington University, so the immediate attention is to help her make a good choice so she can leave home. Meanwhile, she has planned with friends to leave Alaska for a short trip as soon as she graduates this May, and go to Hawaii (the island of Kauai) for a week of backpacking and camping. She did this on her own. She did not ask for any help … only permission. What is a father to do?

Today (and last week, too) Donna and I went cross-country skiing at Kincaid Park, which is tucked in between the airport and the tidewaters of Cook Inlet. It was a wonderful trip but I was distracted by all the tracks I saw in the snow. We have not had much snow since the first of January so I was easily distracted. Many moose tracks—we did not see any moose while skiing—though we did see some while we were driving to the park. Many, many rabbit tracks—we hardly ever see the white snowshoe hares. I do not think that I saw any lynx tracks, but one skier did say that he had just seen a lynx and other skiers reported seeing more. In one spot, there was a mass of ptarmigan tracks. That is unusual in this ski area, but later I was told about an "attack ptarmigan" that would appear by surprise and attack skiers' feet. We saw lots of chickadees and redpolls, magpies and ravens.

When conditions are right, hoarfrost thickly coats everything and transforms Anchorage into another world.

And the mountains and the sunset. The mountain ridges to the west loomed very big on the horizon beyond Cook Inlet. The air was clear and bright. To the north, it was hazy so we could not see Mount McKinley. And along the eastside, the Chugach Mountains streamed from the north to the south. In between, the sun set. This was one of those wonderful brilliant red sunsets and you just wish you could simply sit and watch it change. But, of course, we were skiing and moving along the trail and this in itself created an interesting aspect. Each turn in the trail and each hilltop offered a slightly different and special view of the sunset and the mountains and the inlet. The sky was partitioned in layers of clouds and it became filled with the intense, bright reddish-orange glow of the setting sun. The bright glow was reflected by the snow and trees of the woods around us and the mountains in the background. It was a great time to be out and skiing.

But I digress. You see, although I was enjoying the ski trip, I was befuddled by the observation that my little girl effortlessly skied away ahead of me and took periodic stops to wait for me to catch up. And she started to give me tips on my technique and counsel about how to increase my speed. Didn't she recall that it was I who taught her first how to ski? She giggled as she passed me on a slight hill and recited that she could remember when, as a toddler, she could not get up this hill. I would catch her in front of my legs with my skis outside hers and gently push her up the hill. At least she remembered!

It is simultaneously exciting and disturbing to acknowledge that you can no longer keep up with your offspring. This is both real and symbolic. As skiers, they are stronger. And as they have matured, they have also achieved. You must be pleased and proud with their success—both physically and in maturity as a young adult. But as you see that success, you realize that they have surpassed your abilities to help them and they have become independent and less reliant on your assistance.

I am very proud of the accomplishments of my little girl and I know that she is no longer a little girl and I know that I cannot hold on to her or hold her back, but this does not mean that I must be happy to help send her away from me. We will always enjoy our days together and remember our ski runs and other activities. I wish only the best for her (and for my son, too). This was the revelation that I had today. Revelations are not all that they are cracked up to be. Trust me.

Gotta go. Keep in touch. Love. Bill.

February 14

I had intended to stop with one page, but I am compelled to share some other Alaska observations!

Yesterday morning, I had a meeting with a vendor in downtown Anchorage … at a time when I am not usually in that part of town. At 9 a.m., I happened to look up to the west, over the upper end of Cook Inlet and I was forced to catch my breath. The view was astounding! The sun was just starting to rise up over the mountains on the east side of Anchorage and the Alaska Range on the western horizon was illuminated in a brilliant pink glow. To the northwest, Mount Susitna—Sleeping Lady—loomed larger than usual and also brilliant pink. The air was so very clear. The ridgelines were sharp and piercing. The shadows provided striking contrasts for the brighter colors.

We are lucky, in Alaska, to have so many great views that it should seem easy to have a ho-hum attitude about pretty views, but it does not happen. Every great view is its own reward. Every great view is appreciated and each one is new and special no matter how many times we have already seen it. On this day, I quickly drove up a small hill and parked by the Captain Cook monument and walked out for another, better view. I just admired this bright scene and thought how nice it would be to have a camera. As I was leaving, another person parked and hurried to the viewsite. I turned around and admired the scene again as he shot several minutes of videotape. Our scenery is always beautiful and it is always appreciated.

Early this morning, Karel and I hurried to downtown Anchorage to help with and watch the parade. Today is the first day of our annual Fur Rendezvous (or Fur Rondy) Winter Carnival. Karel did not walk in the parade, but she needed to help a group of her colleagues who were marching to support good nutrition. It was great fun to help and to feel a part of what was happening. And then we discovered two other friends who were also in the parade!

The carnival area of the Annual Anchorage Fur Rondy is a fun place for youngsters.

I must take a break for supper. As I have been typing this, the sun has been setting on another bright, clear day. And the result is just opposite from what I was reporting above … the setting sun is bright and red. The line of Chugach Mountains to the east is illuminated in a brilliant pink glow. The ridgeline is sharp and clear. The shadows are a dark contrast. It is beautiful. We always remind each other to look and see the view. Did you see the Chugach? The Alaska Range! The Talkeetnas! Mount McKinley is out (as it was again, today). Sleeping Lady. Look at the Kenai Mountains! On occasion, neighbors call to say that the aurora borealis, the northern lights, are out tonight! Just wanted to be sure that you don't miss it. Always special!

After the parade, we strolled among the snow sculptures that people and teams have carved into intriguing shapes and messages. Then we drove across town to cheer the start and finish of the second of three heats of the Women's National Championship dog sled race. A fellow state employee, Kathy Frost, is a several-year winner. Kathy won yesterday and today. But after two days of racing, she leads by only two seconds. Tomorrow, Donna and I will probably strap on some snowshoes and walk out to a middle part of the course to do some more cheering today and to get some exercise. We enjoy all seasons in Alaska and there is always something to do—especially during Fur Rondy week.

Mushers in the Annual Anchorage Fur Rondy World Championship Sled Dog Races speed over the 25-mile race course at about 15 or more miles per hour.

February 15

Donna and I had another great day today, watching the mushers as we strolled along on our snowshoes. We were at a spot along the trail that is slightly difficult to get to. The start-finish area is congested and fun in its own way, but here, there were only two race officials and one other observer.

A few other people passed by absorbed in their own activities. We saw the racers emerge from a wooded area, turn, run down one side of an unused runway, make a broad, sweeping turn and return up the other side of the runway, where they made an abrupt turn and swept through a dip in the terrain and disappeared into the woods again. You could see them coming and going and be very close to the track. We had a special treat to see a pair of coyotes cross over the airstrip. Later in the day, we went to the post office and made a stop at Point Woronzof, on the far western edge of the city, high on a cliff overlooking Cook Inlet, rimmed with mountains from the Talkeetnas to the northeast, McKinley to the north, Mount Susitna, Alaska Range with Mounts Spurr, Redoubt, and Iliamna far in the distance. The sun was setting and the mountains were exceptionally clear and bright. The parking lot was filled with cars and many pictures were taken. Skiers streamed by on our Tony Knowles Coastal Trail.

So much to do. So much to enjoy. I hope that you can enjoy this bit of sharing and that you are having a great winter, too.

Love, Bill, Karel, Donna, Bill

January 31, 2008

Oh, wait; there is more … winter is a season of activities in Alaska. Tundra ponds, lakes, streams, and rivers are frozen and snow covered. Traveling is so much easier than during summer, which requires the use of boats or aircraft. Snowmachines and dog sleds skim over the snow, cover long distances, and go directly to a destination. Villagers can readily access other villages to visit friends and relatives and shop or trade. Hunters have access to game. Winter is a busy, active time in Alaska.

The displays of aurora borealis, the northern lights, are dazzling and the night skies become a pleasant, mysterious, undulating pastel glow that reflects off the snow to brighten the night for easier traveling.

Many Alaskans look forward to winter and that includes Alaskans who live in Anchorage. There is so much to do. Just within the city limits, one can ski cross-country or downhill or ski- jump. There are lakes for ice fishing and ice skating areas, indoor and outdoor hockey rinks and sledding hills. Trails are available for jogging, snowshoeing, walking, ski-joring, dog mushing, and even riding snowmachines and horses. In all, Anchorage has over 10,000 acres of municipal parkland with

223 parks and 250 miles of trails and greenbelts. Nearly half of the trails are maintained and groomed for skiing and 24 miles are lighted for nighttime skiing. The Tony Knowles Coastal Trail begins downtown and skirts south along the coast.

Winter in Alaska truly is a busy time that is filled with many activities and enjoyed by most Alaskans. That said, there is even more. If you are bored and not getting out enough ... it's time to Rondy! Even as I type this, I heard another radio advertisement about our annual Fur Rondy.

The 2008 Rondy begins in just two weeks on Friday, February 22 and runs for ten days. Packed into these few days are more activities than you can imagine. It really gets going on Saturday morning with the Grand Parade and that evening a big fireworks display lights up the night. Daily events include the big carnival, complete with rides, food, games, and cotton candy; an art and craft show; pony rides, sled dog rides and helicopter rides; a photo contest; and a melodrama. Karel especially enjoys the massive snow sculptures.

Many races and competitions are scheduled events. The annual World Championship Sled Dog Race begins in downtown Anchorage and is run in three timed, 25-mile heats with a $30,000 purse. Spectators who jam the start-finish chute are likely to see a sprint finish with two or more mushers running down the street with their dog teams. Other spectators prefer to space themselves out on the race course where one can stand very close to the trail for great photo opportunities. Teams play snowshoe softball and hockey and race outhouses. There is the oyster-shucking contest, a SnoCross, ice bowling, and a foot race. Come to the live auction of wild animal hides and horns. And don't miss the Miners and Trappers Ball, or this year, for the first time, the Running of the Reindeer—a short footrace of mixed reindeer and people.

Come for the Rondy; stay for the Iditarod. The Iditarod begins on the second weekend of the Rondy with a ceremonial start on Fourth Avenue, followed by the official timed start from Willow, Alaska on Sunday. Visitors are able to bid for the opportunity to ride with the musher through Anchorage for the casual, relaxed ceremonial start. Spectators line the course and reach out to high-five the mushers. Presently, 99 mushers are signed up to start the 2008 thousand-mile race.

If that is not enough, the twenty-first Tour of Anchorage will be held the next day! This is a 50k (30 mile) point-to-point cross-country ski race across Anchorage that begins partway up the mountain and ends at sea level. It includes several shorter races with classical and freestyle forms.

These are the glorious days of winter in Anchorage. The air is crisp and clear. The days are getting longer and the sun is just beginning its annual work. The gorgeous sunrise serves its reddish-pink glow over the skyline of the Chugach Mountains and against the western sky. In the evening, the sunset returns the shot back against the slope. The shadows and glow of the snow-covered craggy shapes cast a ballet of color and images. As I drove, earlier this week, I turned a corner and faced the mountains in the evening glow. Wow. What a view. I wanted to stop and just watch, but could not. A day later, a thin fog created a subtle filter and the slopes were now a pastel pink and the normally bright blue sky was muted into a soft, milky blue. A few minutes and a mile or two farther, the fog was gone and the familiar panorama returned.

Sadly, over the years, light pollution has invaded the Anchorage bowl and although many people appreciate the security and nighttime visibility, they may not be aware how active the aurora can be. We no longer have neighbors calling to alert us to be sure to see the decorations in the sky.

One last tidbit … the World Championship Sled Dog Races were nearly canceled in 2008 because of lack of snow on the ground; nevertheless, the winter of 2007-2008 was the third snowiest on record.

Link: Anchorage Fur Rondy - http://www.furrondy.net/

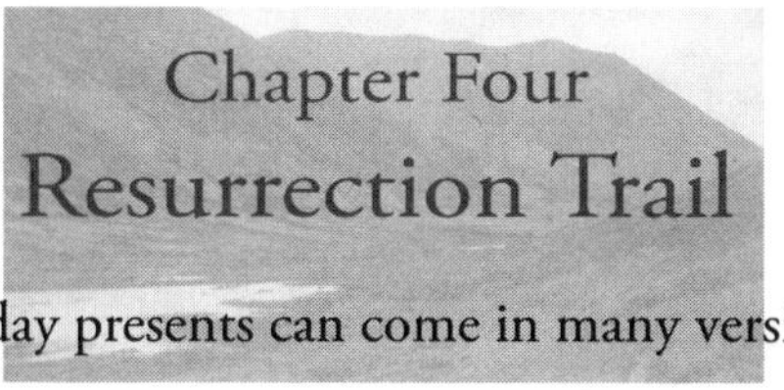

Chapter Four
Resurrection Trail

Birthday presents can come in many versions.

August 15, 1998, 8 a.m.

Good Morning.

Donna and I are off on another adventure. Yesterday, we walked 11½ miles. Only 27 more miles to go in our backpacking hike. She says that this is my late birthday present. It is still too early to tell if I will like it, but I think I will.

As I write, I am lying in my sleeping bag in our little tent beside a noisy, rushing mountain stream, Fox Creek, which pours down into Resurrection Creek. We are hiking the Resurrection Trail. Thirty-eight miles. The trail crosses the spine of the Kenai Peninsula between the town of Hope on the Turnagain Arm of Cook Inlet and Cooper Landing beside the Kenai River. A hundred years ago, 15 years before Anchorage was established on the opposite side of Turnagain Arm on Ship Creek, Hope was a busy town of 5,000 to 10,000 gold-miners. It was the logistics center for the gold fields along Resurrection Creek while the trail, itself, connected Hope and Seward. This trail is old by Alaska standards, but these days, it has become a very popular hiking trail that is shared with mountain bikers, mountain runners, and horseback riders. In winter, it is used by skiers, snowshoers, and snowmachiners.

Donna has a tight work schedule so we could not even start until 2 p.m. yesterday but we were packed and ready. We left as soon as she was off duty and hit the road to Hope. Although Hope is only about 10 miles from Anchorage, it is across Turnagain Arm and an hour-and-a-half drive. We started our hike about 5 p.m. and put in nearly 4 hours of walking. We did well enough; we averaged nearly 3 miles per hour even though it was all uphill and our packs weighed around 40 pounds. Not bad for an old guy and a kid.

We are looking forward to being in high country soon. We are, I think, very near the tree line now and Resurrection Pass and Devil's Pass should be pretty country. We hope to cover about 20 miles today and camp beside Swan Lake tonight. So far, no major problems. Just the expected sore feet and muscles.

I think that it is about time to shut down for now and slip out of the tent to get the stove started and heat some water. No telling how much longer Donna will sleep, but I am ready for some coffee. I am anxious to see what is down, or, rather, up the trail.

The Resurrection Trail takes hikers through areas of thick forest and broad, open valleys and the best panoramic views are on the Cooper Landing side of the pass.

August 16, 8:25 a.m.

Only 10 miles to go. If we really wanted to, we could knock that off in just about 3 hours but we will relax a little and take

more time than that. Karel is scheduled to pick us up at 5 p.m. at the south trailhead where the trail intersects the Kenai River. We will need to drive back to Hope to pick up the other car on our way home. Right now, I am trying to avoid getting up while I am waiting for Donna to wake up. It is raining.

Yesterday turned out to be a full, nice, but tiring day. We walked farther than we had intended simply because of how the trail was laid out. Just when we wanted to stop—and we were both tired and quite ready to stop—we discovered that we would have needed to take an extra side loop off the main trail to get to our intended camping site, which also appeared to have no water source. So we put in another hour until we got to this spot. It is nice here; it is just not very special.

We had a wonderful camping location beside this stream. All drinking water must be filtered or purified.

We started in tall timber yesterday, crossed over the top and hiked about 8 miles in alpine tundra before we dropped abruptly back down into tall timber. Trees are nice, but high tundra is so much more exciting and exhilarating to experience and travel through. Big, wide vistas. Long views of distant mountains and meadows. White slabs of snow lingering from last winter tucked coyly into sheltered mountain flanks, teased by the sun into long, narrow, white streaks of cascading water that coalesce into streams that wind downward through the bright green tundra sedges. Clumps of wildflowers add bright specks and splashes of color to the green backgrounds.

Some areas were filled with wildflowers, but I was a little disappointed as I had expected a much better show. The plants, however, do have the appearance of some tinge of frost and I did hear that there may have been a hard frost. Summer is short in high country. Also, we have not seen as much wildlife as I had hoped. We always enjoy seeing wildlife. We were surprised by a family of spruce grouse and the shrill cries of hoary marmots. Some red squirrels and small birds. Moose and maybe caribou tracks along with some bear sign, but no big critter sightings.

This hike has been focused on walking because we had a limited amount of time. Unfortunately, that meant we had to concentrate on the trail. Watch out for rocks and tree roots and be careful where you put your foot. For me, it was even more challenging. I usually gave Donna the lead, and for the follower it was hard to look up and around. I was only a step or two behind so we could talk; but then, I could only see a few feet of the trail at one time. We covered the ground quite easily and we did not need to take many breaks because the gradient, so far, has been quite mellow with only a few steep pitches.

That is not to say that it was easy. At the end of each day, we were tired. Our feet hurt. Donna's more than mine. Last evening, we enjoyed a nice leisurely supper. We carried our stove and the food down to a bridge over the small stream. While we cooked, we were mesmerized as we watched the water flow by and we relaxed in the feel of the gentle breeze which also kept the bugs at bay.

Backpacking meals are very simple to cook: boil water, add hot water to the freeze-dried ingredients, stir, wait a few minutes so it can rehydrate, eat. An extra snack of dried fruit. No cooking skills are needed.

I guess that it is time to get up. My plan is to try to dress quietly and slip out of the tent. I will use my emergency space blanket to set up a small fly. Hopefully, this will make it a little easier to load our backpacks. We may walk a couple miles before we eat breakfast.

Certainly, it will not be so enjoyable to hike in the rain. The big problem is that although your raincoat keeps the rain out, it keeps the steam from your exercise in. Fortunately, it is downhill from here so it should be less effort and we have lots of time to cover the remaining miles. It is a nice, gentle rain. No wind. The hardest part will be getting started.

Bye for now. Talk with you later.

August 18

As I write this, I am in the doctor's office. I have determined that perhaps over the weekend I may have enjoyed Alaska a little too much. In fact, I may have gotten just a little too close to nature. About halfway through our hike—it was on the uphill leg, just below Resurrection Pass—I stubbed my toe on a rock. We were just cruising along and had a good stride going. I looked up at just the wrong time and *bam*! That is one reason why hikers wear trail boots instead of sneakers. Anyhow, I did not think it would be this serious. I would rather not lose the nail from my big toe, but it is all blue and loose and it aches. The doctor just gave me the news that there is an 80 percent probability that the toenail will fall off within a month or two.

Let's see. Some retrospectives. 1. This was a great trip. I have thought about making the hike for some years. Finally, I—no, we—have done it. The Resurrection Trail is a mellow, enjoyable trek, especially as we did it; from north to south. We did not encounter any steep, long uphill pitches. Oh, there were some to the south of the pass, but we hit those going downhill. 2. We saw less wildlife than I had expected, but in the area where I expected to see caribou, most views were obstructed by tall trees along the trail and we did not stop and spend much time scanning the hills when we were in a more open area. Where we should have seen Dall sheep, the mountaintops were obscured by low clouds. 3. I wanted to be dazzled by the show of wildflowers. Some had already gone to seed; some appeared to have been nipped by an early frost. A friend says that this is a poor year for wildflowers all over. 4. The panoramic views from the southern, downhill side of the pass were outstanding. The broad valley of upper Juneau Creek is flanked by steep mountain slopes, and streaks of snow led to white cascades of water that disappeared on the side of the mountain only to reappear transformed into jewel-like, deep green beaver ponds. 5. People. We did not see as many people as I had expected. Fully half of the people we did see were in a 50-mile mountain foot race. They ran from south to north and all finished in one day. The *Anchorage Daily News* reported that the fastest time was 7 hours and 50 minutes; the slowest (besides Donna and me) was 12 hours and 30 minutes. 6. More people; or, rather, ghosts. I am always interested in historical events and I am aware that the Resurrection Trail was used to service the gold-mining fields during the early years of this century. As we hiked, I felt a sense of connection with the miners that I have seen in old photographs and I visualized them trudging along with a heavy load and looking up at the same mountainsides that I saw.

August 21

It has been a week since Donna and I began our jaunt and I thought I would have had this letter mailed by now. It is time to finish this. The week has become rainy and blustery. A few days ago, I guessed that there had been a hard frost on Resurrection Pass and now I am equally certain that the adjacent slopes and mountaintops are white with this year's first snow.

Actually, the weather we had during our trip was just about as good as it could be. It was warm, but never too hot. It rained, but it never poured. It was breezy, but it never blew too hard. If we had gone this weekend, it would have been quite a different story. Cold and soggy.

But now, our gear has been dried out. The tent is folded and put away. Our hiking boots are cleaned and dried and our backpacks are ready to reload for another trip. I am not sure just what it will be, but I am looking forward to it nevertheless. Donna is lobbying for a sea kayaking trip.

I asked her, "What was the best part of the trip?" Immediately, she replied, "Doing it together!" I agree wholeheartedly! Our time together was wonderful. Priceless. We talked and teased. Joked and laughed. Worried and philosophized. Together. We shared the loads. We shared the views, thoughts, ideas, and plans. A truly special, unique time. Together.

Next, says Donna, was the feeling of accomplishment. We were challenged by the distance and the physical and logistical needs. This is a popular hiking trail, but; as we discovered, not many people actually hike the entire length of the trail. An even less traveled portion of the trail continues across the Kenai River and connects with Seward.

A couple of wet, tired, happy hikers at the end of the three-day, 38-mile Resurrection Trail hike across the Kenai Mountains between the historic gold mining towns of Hope and Cooper Landing.

Overall, we averaged 2.7 miles per hour and, in one reach, early the second day, we traveled at 3.1 miles per hour. I suppose that my biggest regret is that we made the crossing too fast. We did not—could not—take the time to stop and enjoy the area and the views as much as we should have. We were constrained by our work schedules and we had just too little discretionary time to slow down and look around. We did not hurry our steps, but we did keep up a comfortable stride and we kept moving along. An extra day, particularly in the alpine tundra of the pass would have made the trip even more enjoyable.

I must stop. I hope you enjoy these bits of stories from Alaska. Summers here are always a challenging and harried time. So much to do. So much to experience and enjoy.

One final comment. My daughter thought that it would be a great treat to hike the Resurrection Trail with me as a different sort of birthday present. It certainly was a special present; but, as it happens, the other special birthday present also turned out to be a loose toenail.

Gotta go!

Love from Alaska.

Bill, Donna, Karel, and Bill, too!

April 7, 2008

Oh, wait, there is more … so many visitors, and newcomers, too, want to sightsee and view the great scenery that we enjoy here in Alaska. Most get in a line with other vehicles and hurry down the highway so they can stop at the first vista, snap some pictures and move on to the next viewpoint. In between, they strain to get a better view as the terrain goes zooming by. Most are not aware that many of those vistas they have photographed may have hiking trails that pass through or around the space.

Alaska is truly blessed with that great scenery, but much of Alaska is also blessed with a great hiking trail system that allows the hiker to have a unique viewing perspective of that scenery. Instead of rounding the corner on a highway and being awed by an in-your-face view, the hiker has the scene revealed one step at a time before being rewarded with a close-up panoramic view. Rather than waiting for a turn to snap a photo, the hiker can usually just go to the best position and frame the best shot without worrying that someone may step in front. Hikers often have additional rewards. Those folks who are zooming down the highway may see wildlife only when it happens to step on or near the roadway, but hikers usually see a wider variety of wildlife from more different angles, in more different settings, and for longer times than the motorists. Many hikes lead directly to a high mountain lake that is cuddled in a deep cirque the sightseer may not even notice. These are not only so very picturesque and pleasant for viewing and picture taking, but they are also a joy to fish. Hiking or backpacking on a mountain trail gives a person a totally different perspective of the countryside.

Fortunately, these hiking trails are not kept secret, but rather, they are widely advertised and shared. Usually, they originate from very accessible trailheads. Most trails are located on state or federal public-use lands in southcentral Alaska. Many are close to Anchorage where most of the people and roads are also found.

There is an array of trails available for virtually every skill level. Paved, low-gradient, multi-use trails abound in the Anchorage bowl and adjacent to portions of the Seward Highway. Long and short hikes of low, intermediate, and higher gradient are sprinkled about. Some trailheads are nearby; some are several hours down the road. Some are simple round trips. Some may have one or more trailheads so the hiker may have the option of a one-way trip. Most are easy to walk or mountain bike. Some are more challenging.

Okay, you might ask, how can you know where to find the trails and what are they like? Not unexpectedly, there is a number of ways to learn about individual trails within the trail system. First, I suggest, start at the Alaska Public Lands Information Center, which has offices in Anchorage, Fairbanks, Ketchikan, and Tok, or visit their web page. They will connect you with state and federal agencies. Each agency and some non profit organizations publish information and maps for their respective recreational areas. A favorite guide for hikes in the Anchorage area is Shawn Lyons' *Walkabout Guide To Alaska* books. These and other sources contain much information about trailheads, trail distance, elevation change, trail profile, important stops along the way, and degree of difficulty. Other hikers can supply valuable information and the Milepost will assist you to find the trailheads.

One last tidbit ... If you plan to hike, don't forget to plan ahead and be properly equipped for the terrain and weather conditions. Learn how to get along with bears. And do not forget to let a responsible person know your plans and where you will be going. Tell them your plan and your schedule. Then, stick to it.

Link: Alaska Public Lands Information Center
http://www.nps.gov/aplic/center/
http://www.publicationconsultants.com/
Walk About Guide #1 The Kenai and Turnagain Pass
Walk About Guide #2 Chugach Mountains
Walk About Guide #3 Palmer and Hatcher Pass

Chapter Five
Summer in Alaska is Always a Busy Time

Summers in Alaska are never long enough to fit everything in.

July 9, 1992

Hey! Hello all.

I have been thinking about you these days. It is time to write again, but I am not really sure how long it may take to get through this letter. The main message: It is summertime in Alaska and the livin' is *not* easy. Now this may seem contrary to conventional wisdom, so let me explain. As I write this, I am waiting for Bill Jr.'s soccer game to start. Karel and Donna will be arriving soon, too, but either Karel or I will split off before the end of Bill's game to take Donna to her game. Most weeks, our Tuesdays through Thursdays go this way. Rush home, scarf a supper, and rush to the next deadline. You know the drill.

Well, I've have made it to Donna's game. They will be starting soon. Bill's team was ahead four to one. I'd rather be fishing. And the garden needs weeding. Strawberries are waiting to be picked. I need to do some patchwork on the driveway and the yard needs mowing again. I'd rather be fishing or backpacking or just on a day hike. A visit to Denali Park would be great. Maybe whitewater rafting. Or fishing for trout, king salmon, sockeye, or coho.

But that is the problem. The summers are just *too short* for all there is to do. We just had a fine stretch of beautiful weather. Lots of sun. The temperatures were 65 to 70 degrees. Deep blue skies. It was awful. It was perfect weather for all of those activities from about 3 a.m. until nearly midnight and some of that daylight had to be wasted on sleep. Even when you are involved in some fun or otherwise important activity, you must accept the fact that although the sun is still high and the weather is fine, you must believe your watch, stop, and force yourself into bed by 11 p.m. so you can get up and go to work the next morning. Meanwhile, it seems as if everyone else is talking about the fish they have caught or a new trail they tried out. They have been biking or off on a sightseeing trip. How are these people able to take advantage of the time and weather and light to do all the things that I wish I could do?

We have already had some company this year for a weekend, but this is just a tune-up for more to come. In a couple days, Karel and Donna will be off on a trip to the Lower 48 states for a week and a half. Meanwhile, my niece, Nancy, and her husband, Jim, will arrive.

We have survived another evening of soccer. Both teams won. Bill was hoping for more playing time and Donna just wanted to score a goal. It was probably too windy for decent fishing, anyhow.

July 18

We have a few minutes still to wait until the play, *Tom Sawyer*, will start. Bill Jr. is Huck Finn. Boy, it has been a busy week, but I was able to get out for about an hour of fishing earlier today. Karel and Donna visited our parents in Wisconsin and Karel is now at a meeting in Minneapolis, while Donna arrived back home late last night. In between, Nancy and Jim arrived last Thursday evening and by 8:30 the next morning they were on the train on their way to Denali Park.

July 28

Let's see, if this is Tuesday, I must be on the Kenai River. Yes! It is an exciting time to be on the river. This week should be the best time of the season to hook up with a trophy-class king, or Chinook salmon. This is the last week of the season and the numbers of fish in the river have been building for two or three weeks. I am here with Nancy and Jim, Nancy's sister, Patty, her husband, Clint, and his buddy, Eric. Actually, just now, I am in my tent trying to relax because I am very tired. The others are off chasing sockeye salmon. The river is getting a huge run this year of sockeye, or red salmon, too. We fished today from 5 a.m. to 5 p.m., mostly for Chinook salmon with only about a 45-minute break for lunch. Unfortunately, we had nothing to show for our efforts, so the others are off still fishing. I stayed back, but I did fish for an hour or so and landed three sockeye.

Now, this may sound like fun, but I didn't get here until 11 p.m. last night after a 3-hour drive hauling the boat. Last Saturday, my buddy and I had put in another long day dipnetting for sockeye salmon and we brought back 25 fish. Meanwhile, our guests had been in Homer on a halibut charter and brought back 200 pounds of fillets. Oh my, we were up till midnight packaging fish and then we were up again at 6 a. m. to go on a great trip to the

Kenai Fjords National Park at Seward. Monday, I had to work late to meet a deadline. I rushed home to eat and get on the phone. Summertime in Alaska just ain't fun! But you know, it wouldn't be too bad if you didn't have to work.

I'm tired. Worn down. I hope I can sleep. The others will be back soon, but we are scheduled to be up again at 4:30 a.m. to honor the king again. Then we need to hurry back to Anchorage to retrieve their dogs from the dog sitter and so I can get to Donna's soccer game. Deadlines for work and deadlines for recreation, too.

The Kenai River is a large glacially-fed river. During winters, when the glaciers are asleep, the water runs low and clear. The surface elevation changes about 10 feet between summer and winter.

August 23

I am off on a trip to Nunivak Island. Tonight another biologist and I will overnight in Bethel before we head to the village of Mercoryuk in the morning. Hopefully, the weather will allow us to get out to our work site at Nash Harbor. That will be 25 miles in an open 22-foot skiff on the Bering Sea. This is a work trip. Oh yeah, remember? Work. Alaskans have to fit in time for that, too.

Actually, this past month has gone by frightfully fast. I have been out on several fishing trips for salmon, but with little success. I gave a lot to our guests, so we have only about four fillets in the freezer. I guess that I will need to get a few good coho to have enough for cooking and smoking. Fortunately, we did have good luck on a halibut trip a couple weeks ago.

Let's see, what else was happening? Bill Jr. was in California touring with a theater group. They saw Shakespeare plays and gave workshops, too. Karel was in Fairbanks on a business trip and I needed to go to Homer on business. Just for fun, I decided to take Donna along. We flew down and went to the Fish and Game Office.

August 28

On the plane from Mekoryuk to Bethel, on our way back from a good trip.

Anyhow. While I was in Homer, Nick, the local biologist, and I discussed several of his projects and other ideas when he abruptly announced, "It's time to go."

He packed us off and we launched his 18-foot aluminum Bayrunner skiff at the mouth of the Anchor River and we headed off into lower Cook Inlet to fish for halibut. We had a few bites, but no takers until Donna hooked into something. She slowly brought it up toward the surface with Nick and me providing lots of encouragement. But it went back down! She stuck with it and worked it back up. Oh no! Down it went again. It was a much nicer fish than we had first expected. Up again. By now, Donna was sweating and struggling so I helped out. Finally, I had to take the rod alone, but by now, the fish, which eventually weighed in at 90 pounds, had accumulated 50 or more pounds of kelp fronds on the line and the tide was beginning to run hard. Oh my. I could barely move the weight. I was so tired.

Nick took us fishing one evening after work and Donna caught a 100-pound halibut that was just about her size.

We filleted the fish. Donna and I kept two nice pieces and shared the rest with Nick and the office staff. It was a good feeling to share the fresh halibut with all those folks. So now we have a good stock of halibut in the freezer, but we are short on salmon and I will need to work this weekend to catch up on some reports.

This coming Tuesday, September 1, is the opening day for moose hunting and I am planning to go out with a friend who has a drawing permit for a cow moose. Duck season also starts that day. I hope I can find some time for that, too. We haven't done any berry picking either this year. And, it is time to start buttoning things up for the season. How does it all get done?

September 21

This is getting terribly complicated. I never thought it would happen this way. Here I am, waiting for another soccer game to start. This time it is Donna's game. Her first in her junior high school career. She had done fine in her Boys and Girls Club league, but of course, she thought she should have done better.

Anyhow, this summer is just about over. We have had termination dust twice already. Termination dust is the first sprinklings of snow in the high country. It is a signal to the summer visitors that it is time to terminate their stay and start to head back to the Lower 48. Last week, we had some flakes at the city level, but none that stayed on the ground.

The game is starting. I gotta go.

October 6

The moose hunting this year was a bust. Actually, it was a bust in more ways than one. We hunted five days and saw not one bull. I got close enough to shoot two cows, but I did not have a permit, so we are still hungry for moose meat. Also, I missed out on duck hunting and coho fishing because of the moose hunting. And, no caribou either.

As I write this, I am on a plane on my way to Juneau and then to Haines for a meeting. In ten days, however, I will be off on a trip of a lifetime. I am going to Cold Bay at the tip of the Alaska Peninsula for some world-class goose hunting. I am really excited about that trip.

Well, this summer is about over and this letter should be too. We had over two inches of snow about a week ago and the lakes have frozen up. Then it warmed up and the snow and ice melted. I covered the boat for the winter and got the snow tires on the car. Footballs are in the air.

It is time to kick back and try to answer the annual question, "Where has the summer gone?" "What happened to all those grand plans?" No moose in the freezer—although I did see a nice bull in the yard yesterday—and not much salmon, either. Fortunately, the garden was small enough that it did not take up too much time.

Anyhow, you get the picture. I am sure that your summers, and probably your winters, too, are just as frantic. There is just too much to fit into the available time. Next summer, it will be different, right? We will plan it better, schedule it better, take more time off work, and hit it right. But, we know it will not be different. Our plans and activities come after the kids and the family and the housework and the company and a vacation trip and more.

We are about to land in Juneau. It is time to put this away and it is time to end this.

Goodbye all. Goodbye to the summer. Let's do it better next year! Okay?

Love, Bill

P.S. I forgot to point out that our summer came to a rather abrupt end this year. Freeze up and snow came early in the Interior. It began to freeze and snow in mid-September; two or three weeks earlier than usual. Moose season ends on September 20 and caribou season goes on a bit longer. Most hunts are accessed by floatplanes or riverboats. The lakes closed up so fast and so early that many planes were frozen in. Other hunters were stranded because the air taxis could not land with floats and the ice was not strong enough to support landing on skis. Riverboats dodged ice floes on the Yukon River as it froze up. Thirty parties did not make it out on time and were stranded out along the river. People, boats, and aircraft could only be retrieved by helicopter, at $500 per hour.

The Anchorage snowfall was not the earliest on record; but nearly so. Now, our reprieve is nice, but how long will it last?

And now we are all beginning to wonder if we will need to go out and kick ash again. Mount Spurr, our local volcano is reportedly starting to wake up and may be getting ready to erupt again. During the last eruption, we had a nice layer of ash. It is nasty stuff. Very abrasive.

See yuh!

Bill

June 20, 2008

Oh, wait, there is more … Over the years, we have hosted many guests who want to visit Alaska. We help them make plans but eventually reality sets in and they are thinking about packing. What should I bring? What clothes will I need? Do I need a winter coat? What about long underwear? Obviously, the answer depends on your activities, the region of the state, and the time of year.

This year, we will host visitors who will arrive in late May. We will tour Denali National Park by bus and Kenai Fjords National Parks by boat. We will take a-half day Chinook salmon fishing charter and visit Homer and Kachemak Bay. Here are my recommendations:

General information: The weather may range from glorious to terrible. June is the driest and sunniest month in southcentral Alaska, but plan for rainy days. Daytime temperatures average in the low 60s, but could be in the 70s. The lowest nighttime temperatures will be in Denali National Park and some nights could be colder than 32°F and the Denali tour is in a heated bus. Usually, a cold wind blows off the glaciers in Kenai Fjords National Park, but the tour boat has a large, warm cabin. Plan to dress in layers and have a small backpack or tote bag to stuff items into. Casual dress is the accepted Alaska fashion. Two smaller-sized suitcases fit into tight spaces more easily than one big one. Soft sided suitcases are easier to stow than hard-sided suitcases.

<u>Everyday Needs</u>

Casual, comfortable, everyday clothing
Pair of shorts and short sleeve top
Swim suit for hot tub or pool
Personal items
Medications
Long-sleeved shirt
Long-sleeved undershirt
Comfortable jeans or slacks
Medium-weight socks
Comfortable shoes
Sweater or pile jacket
Lightweight, but trustworthy raincoat, which doubles as a windbreaker

<u>Touring and Hiking Needs</u>

Camera
Extra film or digital storage chips
Spare batteries
Small binoculars
Lightweight hiking shoes
Light wool socks
Polypropylene sock liners
Backpack or tote bag
Hat or cap
Sunglasses
Small container of sun block

Small container of insect repellent
Water bottle
Denali and Kenai Fjords National Park
Lightweight gloves
Stocking cap
Sportfishing Charter
Low boots
Good raincoat and rainpants

One last tidbit … Alaska is a big state with very different geographic and weather regions. Visitors must decide where and when they will visit and what sort of activities they will do before deciding what to bring and wear. Although casual dress is the rule, there are opportunities to dress up, too, especially in Anchorage.

Link: item –Visitor information about
Denali and Kenai Fjords National Parks
http://www.denali.national-park.com/weather.htm
http://www.kenai.fjords.national-park.com/visit.htm

Section Two—Fish Alaska

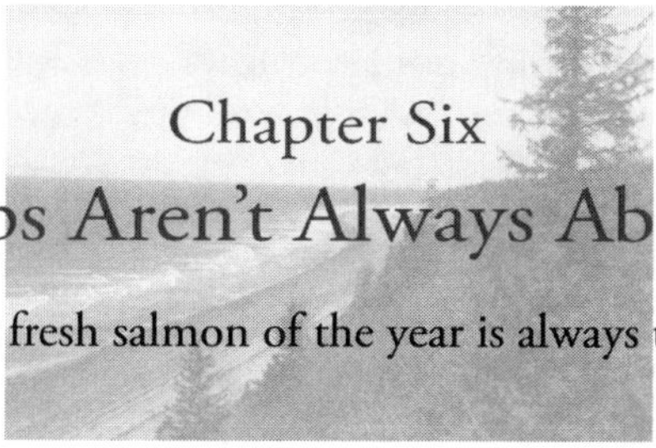

Chapter Six
Fishing Trips Aren't Always About Fishing

The first fresh salmon of the year is always the best.

May, 17 1998

Hello.

Bill Jr. and I returned late last evening from a fun and successful fishing trip that didn't really happen. And we even returned with the first salmon of the year. A king or Chinook salmon. It was a nice fish. Not big. Thirty, perhaps 35 pounds. But it was the first one. And the first one is always the most important.

I had made arrangements several months ago for Bill and me to travel to Homer to meet Nick, a friend and former work colleague, who is now a fishing guide. Nick specializes in trolling for big king salmon in the lower area of Cook Inlet, and in July, when the big kings move into the Kenai River, he goes after them there. He is a very intense fisherman who is recognized by his peers as one of the best. Anyhow, I had planned to have a fun and relaxing campout with Bill and to fish for a day with Bill and Nick to make a nice, full package. But, about a month ago, I abruptly discovered that the weekend we had scheduled to fish was Memorial Day weekend. The fishing wouldn't be bad, but there would be many more boats on the water. And that day, the local streams also opened for salmon fishing, the first big fishing weekend of the year, which means that the campgrounds become overfilled with fishers and campers and cars and dogs and noise and confusion. And there is a good clam-digging tide that weekend, too. This would only increase the dose of overfilled campgrounds and confusion. We changed the trip to this week instead.

We were scheduled to meet Nick at 5 a.m. on Saturday near the mouth of the Anchor River, so we intended to drive to a nearby campsite on Friday to get a nice, leisurely start on the weekend. We planned to set up our tent and kick back, relax, cook a steak for supper and get a good night's sleep. Along the way, we stopped in Soldotna to take a stretch break and we decided that we had lots of time so we went across town to say hello to Loren and Sandra. Loren is another friend and former Alaska Department of Fish and Game colleague who is now a fishing guide on the Kenai River for king and coho salmon. Loren came running to the door still chewing a sandwich and at about the same time, the phone rang. In between, he paused long enough to say "Hey, come on fishing with us. I'm leaving in thirty minutes with a client." Bill and I switched gears fast, got ready to go, and away we went.

The rest, as they say, is history. Loren maneuvered the boat in the current and made the lures work. It was early in the run and few fish were in the river. Mainly, the time was long and boring and cold. We waited. We hoped. Suddenly! We had a hit! The reel screamed, the rod dipped. I grabbed the rod and it pulsed. The fish ran. Hang on. The line went limp. Gone. No! "*Reel!*" Loren knew what had happened. The fish had turned and was running just as fast right back toward us! "Reel!" I felt it again. Abruptly, it was over. A nice fish. Not a big king. But a nice fish.

Above all, it was the first fish. The first salmon of the season. We had chatted about keeping fish and how long they would last in the freezer. I did not realize that here in my hands was such an extraordinary fish. This was only a small king. Not a big king. It was a nice king, but above all, it was *the* king. The first of the year. The brightest, the biggest, the best, the unique. The first king of the year. It took me a while to realize (along with some urging from Loren) what a special prize I had attained, but slowly, I began to realize that this particular fish, which happened to be one of only eight known to be caught on the river on this day, was special. It needed to be shared. Its value as the first special meal of long-missed succulent, fresh salmon far exceeded its value as a collection of frozen lumps of fish flesh in a freezer. It begged to be shared. I was pleased that this one modest fish was transformed into a special meal and a special sharing that extended from our family to Loren's and his children's family and to the other clients as well. We simply are so blessed here in Alaska that it is easy to enjoy the bounty and to be able to share it so easily.

Bill and I finally left Soldotna at about 10 o'clock in the evening. With luck, we managed to find a No-Name Diner that was still open on the outskirts of the metropolis of Ninilchik, where we had an overly generous meal of barbecued ribs and potatoes. We were the last diners and they were glad to empty the pan.

We set up the tent in the dark and the rain at Stariski Creek Campground. This was not feeling like the nice relaxing trip that we had planned.

The alarm clock rang a mere four hours later. We dragged out. Not fun. Trudge to the meeting place near the Anchor River. Another truck. A phone call from Nick who was calling from Homer. How strong is the wind? What angle? Can we fish today? How is the surf? Safe conditions? No! Just not right. No fishing today. Bill and I headed back to our camp and back to bed.

We enjoyed a fine view of Cook Inlet from the edge of the cliff at the Stariski Creek Campground.

About 11 a.m., Bill and I got out of the tent. We cooked and shared a brunch of hot cider, coffee, caribou sausage, and fried potatoes. We drove to Homer for a surprise visit with Nick and Norma. Although the water was too rough to fish, Nick was getting ready for his next trip. He was animated and his excitement was infectious as he took nearly an hour to show and demonstrate all the special features he had installed on his boat, a 20-foot Bayrunner. Autopilot, global positioning system, depth sounders—one down looking and another side-looking. Norma supplied fresh hot chocolate chip cookies. Easy load; easy off trailer. More cookies. Special spinners. Bright lures. New rods, reels. Very comfortable boat. And we never left the driveway!

Mount Redoubt, an active volcano, dominates the horizon across Cook Inlet from the Kenai Peninsula.

After this experience, Bill Jr. decided to adjust his definition, upward, of the term "die-hard fisherman."

We said goodbye to Nick and Norma and returned to our campsite at Stariski Creek. We picked up our tent and other gear and we cleaned up our site. But before we left, we took the time to just sit and look and enjoy the view. The wind was still strong, but the air had cleared. The view of the mountains of the Alaska Peninsula was panoramic. Mount Redoubt and Mount Iliamna were the main jewels of the chain. Waves and surf crashed on the beach 200 feet below at the base of the cliff. Behind us were the moribund tops of 40-foot spruce trees that were being killed by the little spruce bark beetles. In between, bald eagles cruised and rode the air currents. Juvenile eagles tested their wings. Adults with their brilliant white heads and tails peered at us with their sharp, yellow, judgmental eyes.

We drove back to Anchorage. We talked. We listened to music. Bill Jr. tried to explain the music to me. We watched for moose and other hazards. A sign that warned "Brake for Moose" said that nearly 300 had been killed on this road this year. We saw nearly 30 moose on this trip, alone. While we were on the Kenai River, we had seen other moose, caribou, more eagles, an otter, and other mammals and birds. The air was exceptionally clear and clean. Mountains were sharp, clear, and white in brilliant contrast with the deep blue sky and the dark shadows of the slopes, the green of the trees and the angle of the light.

We often see eagles when we travel on the Kenai Peninsula but we never get tired of seeing them. We have one or two fly over our house in Anchorage several times a year.

The views of the mountains and the rivers and the trees and the other scenery were spectacular. Every turn of the road displayed another view and more scenery. All were beautiful. Each was as breathtaking and special as the one last seen and each one was better than the one last seen. We had counted over 30 eagles beside the road in Turnagain Arm as we traveled south. Dipnetters were busy and very active as they fished for hooligan, a smelt-like fish.

It was a great day! And a great trip. We just enjoyed the views and the music and the discussions and the time together and the greatness of Alaska. We reveled in the opportunity to share one small, special fish. We had reversed the hectic start to the relaxing trip that we had planned. We just decided that we were lucky to have that fish to share and that we had had a special fishing trip even though we never did go on the trip we had planned. The fishing trip that wasn't.

Gotta go. Love.

Bill and Bill Jr.

P.S. The sharing continues. A neighbor, Dave, "borrowed" a couple bags of eggs from this fish that I had cured for bait. He will be going fishing for kings this weekend, and when he is successful, he will repay with more eggs and with *fresh-smoked king salmon.*

March 15, 2007

Oh, wait, there is more ... Chinook or king, salmon are prized by many Alaskans. They are the earliest of the salmon species to return to freshwater from the ocean to spawn. And of course, they can be big. Chinook salmon are the largest of the five species of Pacific salmon in North America. The largest known Chinook salmon weighed 126 pounds. It was caught in a fish trap near Petersburg, Alaska in 1949. The world record for a sport-caught Chinook salmon is 97 pounds 4 ounces, caught by Les Anderson from the Kenai River in 1985. Actually, I was fortunate to be in Soldotna on that day working with Loren and he took us to view the fish. It certainly was impressive. Mr. Anderson stood and cradled the fish with both arms while the spectators clicked their shutters and admired the fish until he asked quietly, "Can I put it down now?"

Actually, there are two runs of Chinook salmon in the Kenai River. Fish in the late run, which peaks in July, weigh more, on the average, than those in the early run, which peaks in June.

The life cycle of Chinook salmon in southcentral Alaska begins with spawning in midsummer. The eggs incubate in the gravel and the inch-long, feeble fry, or alevin, hatch in late winter, but remain in the gravel until their yolk sac is absorbed. The fry wriggle up and out of the gravel and become free swimming soon after the ice breaks up.

The fry live and grow in the river for one year. They usually live in a narrow band of slow-moving water along the shoreline where tree branches and other natural woody debris create places to hide while they wait for the current to bring bits of food. They eat aquatic and terrestrial insects, but when postspawning salmon begin to die, the young fish have an excessive feast on the pieces of fish flesh. The abundance of nutrients is invaluable for the fry because they need to store energy to survive the winter and because, soon after winter, they will transform into smolts and begin their downstream migration to the ocean.

Chinook salmon usually spend between one and four years in the ocean, probably making a circular migration of the North Pacific Ocean each year. As they migrate, they eat mostly fish while they grow and mature. A small percentage of those from each "smolt-year" population of migrants return to the stream after one year as miniature, but functional, adults. A higher percentage return after two years and most return after three years. A small proportion of Chinook salmon from some streams, such as the Kenai River, return after five or even six years at sea. Longer time at sea means more feeding and more growing.

Adult Chinook salmon do not feed after they return to freshwater and they die after they spawn, as do all anadromous Pacific salmon. However, again, as with all anadromous salmon, the dead bodies make a huge contribution to the river ecosystem. Young salmon, trout, and scores of predators and scavengers feed on the decomposing carcasses. Nutrients are released into the water where they become fertilizer to stimulate the base of the food chain as well as seep into the groundwater which stimulates the growth of trees and other vegetation in the riparian zone.

Some ecologists are fond of saying that salmon swimming upstream are not really fish, but rather bags of fertilizer with fins moving upstream carrying huge amounts of nutrients derived from marine foods that will be used to fertilize the otherwise sterile waters that originated as snowmelt and rain.

One last tidbit ... Yukon River Chinook salmon are considered by many the tastiest and most succulent salmon of all because they have a high fat content. These salmon may migrate 2,000 miles in the ocean and 2,000 miles up the river and into Canada to spawn.

Links: Kenai Peninsula information; the Alaska Outdoor Journal
http://alaskaoutdoorjournal.com
ADF&G Wildlife Notebook Series, Chinook salmon
http://www.adfg.state.ak.us/pubs/notebook/fish/chinook.php

Chapter Seven
Let's Go Fishing, or Hunting

I think that the word *multitasking* was just entering my vocabulary in the early 1990s, but we sure did it on this fishing trip.

September 15, 1995

Hey. Hello.

I just decided that I had to tell you about my recent fishing trip. Besides, I have some time to kill just now. I am caught in the same situation that you have heard before. Yup, I'm weathered in again. But this time it is different because I am at home. I was scheduled to go out on a caribou hunt this morning at 9 a.m. (it is now 2:30 p.m.), but the weather is so bad that I have not yet departed to the air taxi service. Maybe we can start in another hour or tomorrow morning.

The fishing trip. It is one of those stories that usually starts out "Only in Alaska …" It began simply enough. My longtime frequent fishing buddy, Joe, says, "Let's go get some coho salmon. It's late in the season and we both still need some fish for the freezer."

Major highways in Alaska are numbered, but Alaskans use names as identifiers. The Parks Highway travels between Wasilla, which is near Anchorage, to Fairbanks. Willow Creek is one of many nice fishing streams that cross the Parks Highway.

"Okay, where?"

"Rabideaux Slough."

The Rabideaux Slough is a drive of about 2½ hours north of Anchorage on the Parks Highway. "I'll pick you up at 5 a.m." Groan. But wait. Moose season has just opened. "Maybe we should take a rifle, just in case."

"Okay."

At 5:30 a.m., Joe calls. "I'm just leaving now. By the way, do you have a harvest ticket permit to shoot a moose? Do you know what is legal in that area?"

Seven o'clock. We stop in Wasilla to get a cup of coffee, a donut, a harvest ticket, and the regulations.

Head north, toward the Susitna River. It is a pleasant, quiet drive. We are almost to our destination with 10 miles to go and finalizing our fishing plans and strategy for the day. You won't guess what happened next.

I saw a dark shape by the left side of the road, about 100 yards off. Double take. A *bear*! A black bear. Another look. It is a nice-sized bear in excellent condition–not huge, but very nice. "Should we stop?"

"I dunno."

"Do you want to take it?"

"Should we go back?" By this time, we are at the turnoff from the highway to the slough.

"Why not, we really should at least give it a try."

Turn around. "Wait. Do you need a harvest ticket to shoot a black bear?" "How far from the road do you need to be?"

Do you get this picture? Here are two long-term State of Alaska Fish and Game biologists who qualify for sourdough status, driving back down the road looking for a black bear, distracted from their fishing trip. The driver is eyeballing the road and the roadside for a sign of this great quarry. The other guy is frantically paging through the hunting regulation book to determine if they can legally take the game and how far off the road they must be to pull the trigger. This almost sounds like a scene out of an Abbot and Costello movie, doesn't it?

Well, needless to say, the black bear was not seen again. That ended our hunting for *this* fishing trip. Actually, it was kind of an omen. In fact, it was the high point of the trip. The slough was an interesting fishing area, but it was not terribly pretty. The water was low and the fishing was boring. There was virtually no action. Slowly, all the other parties left. Hey, what a deal, we had the spot all to ourselves. "Can we leave now, too?"

Actually, we did catch some fish. We didn't get skunked. I held the high rod for the day—with two small burbot. Oh, boy. (Burbot go by many names—ling, ling cod, lawyer, eelpout, more.)

Joe didn't want to take any and the fillets from both amounted to only about 1½ cups of meat. Karel and I were delighted to try something new and we were not disappointed. It was delicious.

Excellent views of Mount McKinley are periodically presented from the Parks Highway.

So, although our fishing plans didn't work out very well, and although we were on the wrong side of success as bear hunters, we had a great trip and a nice, tasty meal, too.

Only in Alaska …

Now, if the weather clears, maybe we can get on with our caribou trip. We plan to be gone nearly a week. I plan to write and tell you about that trip, also.

Mainly, my summer has been good. Terribly hectic, both at home and at work. Many little tasks. Many interruptions. I had house repair work that had to be done before I could paint. And I wanted to dig up some flowerbeds, but not before the painting. And I still have insulation work to do too. Some people argue that there are only two seasons in Alaska. *Winter* and *Getting Ready for Winter*. Sometimes I believe it.

Donna was a starter on her soccer team again this summer and we went to most of the games. That sure eats into the fishing time. Now she is involved in high school cross-country running and will be in classes by the time I return from the caribou trip. She is presently doing some practice driving in a class, too. Bill is working at a gift shop while he is waiting anxiously to start college at the University of Oregon in a couple of weeks. Karel is working today, too. She has been quite uncomfortable lately with a slight herniated disk between two neck vertebrae. Hopefully, this will clear up sooner rather than later.

I have decided that I don't want to grow any older. I will be back from my hunt for a week before I have to go to Oregon with Bill for his start-week; then nonstop meeting and training till the end of the September. By mid-October, snow. Maybe it is time to get ready for winter.

It was good talking to you again. Think about you a lot. Wish we could be closer, but we still enjoy Alaska and all the Great Land has to offer—talk with you later.

Love,

Bill

March 2, 2007

Oh, wait, there is more ... I don't just write letters. I have been writing a column called "FISH TALK" for a number of years. It is about fish biology and it appears in the monthly newsletter for our local fly-fishing club, the Alaska Fly Fishers. As it happens, I once wrote a FISH TALK article about burbot. Here it is.

Codfish in Lakes. Have you ever gone fishing for cod? Have you ever gone fishing for cod in *freshwater*? This may seem like a pretty silly question because we all know that marine fish cannot survive in freshwater. Actually, this is sort of a trick question because one member of the cod family really *does* live in freshwater. In fact, you may have caught a true cod in freshwater and never have known it. Few people know about this little fun fact because the fish is not called a cod. Meanwhile, there are other fish that may be called cod, but they are not.

The "freshwater cod" is often overlooked, and in many areas people may not even know or care that it exists. In some areas, however, it is well known and greatly appreciated. The misunderstanding begins with its name. It goes by many common names: eelpout, lawyer, spineless catfish, cusk, ling, ling cod, freshwater lush, and probably others, too; but the accepted common name is "burbot."

First, the scientific name for burbot is *Lota lota*. I love the way that name makes my tongue roll and I must tell you a little story that goes along with that name. While I was in my last year of college, I was helping some graduate students to collect and study fish from a small lake in northern Wisconsin by electroshocking. One night we captured a goodly number of fingerling-sized burbot which we put into our holding tank. We giggled about how we had "caughta lotta little *Lota lota*." Say it fast. Doesn't that just make your tongue warble? Sorry, I get distracted easily.

Burbot are easy to recognize. They are long and slender, with two dorsal fins; the first is very short but the second extends over most of the back half of the body. The anal fin is nearly as long. Burbot are generally dark with a blotchy pattern on the top and sides and pale yellow or white below. As with all true codfish, they have one prominent barbell, or feeler, at the tip of the lower jaw.

Burbot are found in the northern latitudes around the world, usually in lakes, but also in deep holes in large rivers. They live on the bottom, commonly in deep areas, but they move into shallower water at night to feed. After they grow longer than 5 to 6 inches, they feed predominantly on fish, but they are not very selective.

Spawning occurs in midwinter, at night, under the ice where the water is about 1 to 5 feet deep (sometimes, up to 30 feet.). There is no pairing and the fish form a great milling mass over clean gravel and stones where eggs and sperm are released. Burbot mature at as young as 2 to 4 years near the southern part of their distribution, but as much as seven years farther north. An average female will lay about 600,000 small eggs but large females may have nearly 1.5 million. After the eggs are fertilized, they settle to the bottom and develop without any attention or care from the parents. Newly hatched fry begin life only about 3/16 inch long.

Growth depends on both good feeding conditions and good water temperature. Those near the southern part of their range generally grow faster than those from the north. Although burbot rarely live longer than 15 years, one 24-year-old fish from interior Alaska was nearly 40 inches long.

In much of the United States, burbot are not well known and have been largely overlooked. Early explorers in the Canadian arctic ate it only as a last resort, and over much of its range it is not eaten. In Alaska, however, it is often sought after, especially by ice fishermen. I have heard some people say that they prefer the flavor of burbot to that of halibut.

One last tidbit … most members of the cod family are marine fish but some species are found in brackish waters and estuaries.

Link: ADF&G Wildlife notebook series, Burbot
http://www.adfg.state.ak.us/pubs/notebook/notehome.php

Chapter Eight
Karel's King

King, or Chinook, salmon always attract
special attention and require special effort.

July 24, 2003

Hi all.

Well, it has been a busy week on the Kenai River.

Summer in Alaska is always a busy time and it is even more so when people are visiting. Bill Jr. was here, but he returned to New York City a couple weeks ago. Donna and Peter were down to their last week before she would need to return to Seattle to begin her research studies in Puget Sound on killer whales, which will lead to a master of science degree, and Peter would head out to Bristol Bay for a 7-week class and research that focused on sockeye salmon. So, of course, Donna and Peter borrowed our car to spend three days sea kayaking in Kachemak Bay. They returned on Monday.

On Tuesday, they and I loaded up and headed to Soldotna, where we set up camp and met Dean, a work colleague and friend, who is a skilled and avid fisherman for Chinook salmon in the Kenai River. We had such a fun and relaxing evening fishing and talking and basking in the lowering sun, which was still up at 10 p.m. when we stopped fishing. Our relaxation was rudely interrupted several times by something pounding on the line and "burying" the rod tip. Peter landed—but released—a nice 40-pound class Chinook salmon. Donna hooked a small 20-pound Chinook which we also allowed to swim away. We had another fish on which was the size of Peter's fish, but it detached itself before we had a good look. It was a wonderful evening and a great experience. Thank you, Dean.

But Peter had not had enough … I crawled into my tent. Peter went back to fishing from shore. Two hours, one sockeye.

We were up at 5 a.m. on Wednesday. A quick, simple breakfast. And we were on our way to the mouth of the Kenai River where we planned to start at high tide to dipnet for sockeye salmon. This fishery is available only to Alaska residents and at only a few locations. Our legal limit was a total of 90 fish for the two families, but our personal limit was only about 20 between us.

We peered over the beach berm at 6 a.m. and saw 6- to 8-foot swells breaking on the beach. We did not even gear up. We relocated and tried another location for an hour. No luck. The fish were there, but our net handles were too short. Skunked. Disappointed.

Our dipnets had a 15-foot handle attached to a 3-by-4-foot frame hung with gill net mesh. These are fished by holding the net in the current until a fish runs into it.

We went back to the mouth of the river. Swells were still breaking on the outer beach, but we decided to try a more upstream, semiprotected part of the beach.

It was unbelievable. We caught 24 fish in one hour. That is about one fish every 5 minutes in each net. As good as it gets. Later, we learned that nearly 90,000 sockeyes entered the river that day and 130,000 the next. Most of our catch went immediately into the freezer, some went into the smoker, and some directly onto the charcoal grill.

Personal use dip-net fishing for salmon is an uniquely Alaska experience. As with any fishing, you need to be at the right place and time but when the fish are in it becomes organized chaos.

Friday after work I turned around and headed back down to the Kenai River with Karel. Saturday at 6 a.m., we started fishing for Chinook salmon. At 9 a.m., Donna boarded her plane. Noon, Peter boarded his. By that time, we had already had a great day on the river. We were out with Loren, a retired Alaska Department of Fish and Game biologist, now a fishing guide, and a friend. We always enjoy our trips with Loren and schedule one every year. We were out with two other fishers who were visiting from Hawaii and we all had tales to tell in between the interruptions. Collectively, we caught one in the

60-pound class, one in the 45-pound class, three in the 20-pound class, and one in the 16-inch class. We kept the two largest.

Loren nets a king salmon for Karel. The Kenai River hosts both an early run and a late run of Chinook or king salmon. The average size of late-run fish is larger than the early-run fish.

Karel scored big. Her fish was just under 60 pounds. Forty-five inches long. A big male. She did a good job. I guess she usually comes along to keep me company and enjoy a relaxing ride on the river. This day, she could really relax after she boated this one, because the rules say that you cannot continue to fish from a boat after you keep one king. Karel hung in there and worked the fish in—with the help and skill of Loren. She wore herself and the fish out and she was glad it was over. I reminded her that if she released the fish, she could keep fishing and catch another. "No!" she cried out. "This is enough! No more!"

Loren displays Karel's 45-inch, 60-pound king salmon from his decking on the bank of the Kenai River.

Oh ... the king I caught was somewhat smaller than 60 pounds.

Sunday, we returned to Anchorage via a short detour through Homer. It was another beautiful day. Some rain. We enjoyed the wonderful viewscape and we enjoyed a good visit with Nick and Norma. Nick is also a retired Alaska Department of Fish and Game biologist and friend, who is recovering from a nerve/muscle problem with his leg. He is doing well, but it is a difficult time for him because his serious fishing plans for the summer were thwarted. But it was good to see him and Norma and chat a bit before the long trip home.

We arrived home about 8 p.m. Sunday evening.

It was a very busy week on the Kenai River.

Hope your summer is going well. Let us know what is happening.

Keep in touch.

Bill and Karel

Oh, wait, there is more ... the Kenai River is quite a remarkable river. It is an amazing fish production factory. By most standards, it is not a large river and it does not have an extensive drainage area, but it does include several lakes, two on the mainstem itself.

All five species of North American Pacific salmon return to the river to spawn while rainbow trout and Dolly Varden reside in the river and most of the tributaries, along with other native fishes. Of the salmon, the Chinook salmon receives special attention because it is the largest. Sockeye salmon, however, also receive special attention because they are more abundant and provide excellent table fare. Coho salmon are generally considered to be the feistiest of the salmon. Pink salmon are the smallest of the North American Pacific salmon and their in-river abundance varies greatly from one year to the next. Run strength during even-numbered years is much greater than during odd-numbered years. Chum salmon are the least abundant salmon in the Kenai River.

Both the Chinook and sockeye salmon have two spawning runs in the Kenai River. The early run of each peaks in June and second run peaks in July. Early-run fish tend to spawn in higher and colder tributaries whereas the late runs tend to spawn in the river mainstem and in tributaries below lakes. The second-run fish tend to have a larger average size.

The Kenai River drainage has produced State of Alaska sportfish record-Chinook (97 pounds, 4 ounces), sockeye (16 pounds), and pink salmon (12 pounds, 9 ounces). The Chinook salmon is also the sportfishing world record. Interestingly, this fish was caught in mid-May; not in July.

This abundance of salmon, of course, supports commercial, sport, subsistence, and personal-use fisheries. The commercial fishery and some sport fisheries take place in Cook Inlet where salmon destined to enter the Kenai River are mixed with salmon which are headed to other streams and it is difficult to impossible to ascribe harvests to a particular spawning river; nevertheless, the Kenai River is the largest producer of salmon in Cook Inlet and the average annual Cook Inlet commercial harvest of all salmon in recent years has averaged about six million fish.

Most importantly, the primary mission of biologists who are responsible for salmon management in Alaska is to assure that enough adult fish reach the spawning grounds to maintain strong return in future years. Each year, the managers make a forecast for the following summer's run strength and, during the season, they assess the run strength as the fish return. The intensity of the fisheries is adjusted in season depending on the numbers of fish that are reaching the spawning grounds.

After the salmon enter freshwater they encounter an intensive sport fishery, perhaps the largest sport fishery in the state. The intensity is enhanced because it is located adjacent to the population and commercial center of Alaska and it is easily accessed from the road system.

Chinook salmon are highly prized and an average of about 17,500 are harvested annually from the Kenai River by anglers, the largest Chinook salmon sport fishery in Alaska. About 41,000 coho salmon are harvested by sport anglers each year, also the largest coho salmon sport fishery in the state. The 20-year average annual total run strength for sockeye salmon in the Kenai River is 3.7 million fish, of which, an average of about 240,000 are harvested by anglers.

Personal-use fisheries are unique to Alaska and are only for Alaskans. Personal-use dipnetters have harvested an average of nearly 290,000 salmon from the Kenai River in recent years. Most are sockeye salmon. A small number of salmon are also harvested by subsistence fishermen.

Resident species of rainbow trout and Dolly Varden support a large–and growing–sport fishery that is managed mostly with catch-and-release regulations. Nearly 100,000 rainbow trout and over 110,000 Dolly Varden are caught annually from the Kenai River by anglers.

Many resident and visiting sport, commercial, personal-use, and subsistence fisherfolks take advantage of the bounty of five species of salmon and several resident fishes in the hard-working Kenai River each year.

One last tidbit. Between 1997 and 2006, the Kenai River drainage supported an average of 386,500 angler days of sport-fishing effort and 17,400 fishing days of effort in the personal-use dipnet fishery.

Link: More on Kenai River fisheries
http://www.cf.adfg.state.ak.us/region2/finfish/salmon/uci/kenairiver.php

Chapter Nine
A Family Fishing Adventure

The definition of a fishing trip has nothing to do with catching.

May 6, 1994

Hello.

Surprise! Another letter. And I am not even in an airplane or an airport or weathered into some remote place waiting for a pickup. I am in my nice warm office. But I have been thinking of all sorts of things, so I decided to get a headstart on this letter that I knew I would write sooner or later.

Here's the situation. My brother, Jim, his son, Nick, and my dad will arrive in Anchorage in about a month for a weeklong fishing trip. My son, Bill, may join us for all or part of the time, but he has not yet settled on his summer schedule. I am the chief planner and organizer.

This job of outfitter for such a trip is really quite awesome. Visitors from the Lower 48 rarely have a good concept of what to expect before they get here and do not have a good selection of the right equipment. So, how do I get it together?

I query, "What do you want to fish for?"

"More fish is better than bigger fish but we'd like to fish for halibut, too."

"When will you come?"

"First half of summer."

Okay. That means June. The tides are good for halibut between June 10 and 18. My favorite charter boat is available only on June 15, so everything will swing around that date. We will have only one week and one of the days will be for halibut in Homer. That means we will be on the Kenai Peninsula all week. Our main salmon target will be Chinook or king salmon. These will be the early-run fish, which average smaller than the late-run fish. Usually around 18 to 35 pounds; rarely 45 pounds.

What else? Lodging, gear, reservations. I started calling people, tying flies, checking my equipment, making lists, asking questions, and finalizing plans.

June 25

As you can see, I haven't made much progress. Actually, I had done a bit more typing on this, but as I was saving the file, the disk failed. I lost all that I had typed. It wasn't very much, but at least it was more than this. Nevertheless, I could use that typing now because I am not making much progress here. I am watching a television movie as I try to write and I am doing more watching than writing.

June 27

At the rate I am going, you may never hear this story. As I said earlier, I wanted to have everything in order; and, just when I thought I had everything under control, Bill Jr. discovered that he would be able to join us for the first part of the trip. So I changed the halibut charter to include him. Then he decided he could join the whole trip, so I changed the other parts of the trip, too. Such is the life of an outfitter.

When my Dad arrived, I had things pretty well ready to go. On Friday, he and I went to pick up the little camper trailer that I had rented. Dad got it loaded up and we were ready for Jim and Nick when they arrived that evening. After blueberry sourdough pancakes for our Saturday breakfast, we were off. The great Alaska fishing adventure had begun. Salmon fishing! Halibut! Rainbow trout! Camping!

Many good camping sites are readily available on the Kenai Peninsula.

What happened? You can guess. *No fish!* Well, nearly no fish. We saw lots, but caught few. Nonetheless, we had a great trip. We had a wonderful time. It was great to simply be together all week. Grandpa, his two sons, and their sons. A special, wonderful trip.

We started well. Jim landed two nice kings, one about 30 pounds. The plan was working. We had a great campsite. Dad, Jim, and I shared the camper. Bill and Nick had a big tent for themselves and they talked for hours. We saw lots more kings, but we caught no more.

We boarded our halibut charter on Wednesday, excited and ready to get some of the big fish. Another disappointment. We were blown off the water before we could even get to the fishing grounds! We managed to reschedule a half-day trip with another operator on Thursday. This time, we never got out of the parking lot because of the wind.

We relocated our camp and went after sockeye salmon in the Russian River. It was a long hike, but we couldn't locate many fish. It was tough fishing. Again no luck! I was depressed and frustrated. With all of our planning, our expectations and high hopes were in shambles.

You and I and everyone else know that no one can control the fish or the weather but you and I also know that we always want to have the best of everything for our guests. It just didn't work out.

Fortunately, the weather was good—except for those two days of wind. The food was abundant and the comradeship was wonderful. And all of this was fertile ground to sprout some famous quotes and great stories.

At the height of my frustration and disappointment, Bill Jr. worked hard to cheer me up. He said, "Why is everyone so uptight? This is just a fishing trip. I don't care if I catch fish." He is wonderful. He enjoys the social aspects so much that he will make a special effort to join the trip even though he really may not care very much about fishing or hunting.

In fact, during the trip Bill was a bit of a pied piper as he practiced his saxophone. That's right. His sax. He brought his sax in case he became bored with fishing. The rest of us were not bored. We were always fishing, getting ready to go fishing, eating, or sleeping because we were tired from fishing. Bill didn't fish quite as hard as the rest of us and found time to practice jazz on his sax. The melodies were great as the sound floated over the campground, but soon he was interrupted by a visitor who came to chat about the music. Later, the visitor returned to introduce his daughters and his whole family. At the streamside, a few moments of playing attracted another young lady who was also a music student. That was a bummer. A short practice.

Another quote. By Nick:"At first, we strained to get a good look at every eagle that was near. After a few days, it was … oh, just another eagle." I thought it was just great. It is so nice to be able to share a bit of Alaska.

Our last day of fishing was a guided trip on the Kenai River. We didn't catch any sockeyes, but we got some nice—though not large—rainbow trout and Dolly Varden. This was when we learned that those small round floating things attached to your fishing lines may be called "bobbers" ... but if you have a fly on the end of your line, they are called strike indicators.

Drift boats are an excellent means to access the best fishing holes for rainbow trout, Dolly Varden, and sockeye salmon on the upper Kenai River. They work well for transporting anglers ... and sleeping, too.

Dad was a great trooper! He said that he wasn't sure that he could walk very well, but he never quit. He was involved in everything. All the time. He seemed to get stronger as the week went on. I think that we should do this again so we can all enjoy it all over again so he—and all of us—can be rejuvenated!

Bill Jr. writes: The trip really did go pretty well. I did bring my sax, and played because I enjoy it. Dad's assumption of my noninterest in fishing is a little off. I'm not quite the die-hard guy he is; I just like to have a balance. I couldn't play my sax all the time; I'd take a break and go fishing. So, altogether, we had a good time. Although the mosquitoes were bothersome, the weather couldn't have been much better, except for a little wind. But that was just a little confusing.

The views everywhere were really cool, and even if we didn't catch a lot of fish, we had plenty of adventures. Such as the stranding of three fishermen. It started out harmless enough when Jim, Nick, and I waded to a little island to fish from. But Jim's instincts saved the day! He noticed the rising tide and got us off the island before we would have been stranded there until the tide went out. Nick and I managed to get to shore dry, but only barely. But sensing the hopelessness of the situation, Jim plunged into the water with reckless abandon, and that evening he was cooking his socks and pants over the campfire. He was a little wet. Commenting on his dinner, Jim said "Mmm … really salty. A little tough. I hate soggy food! Geez … that's a lot of salt. I sure wish I hadn't done that." Well, we all felt bad, and the first rule never to be broken was that we wouldn't tease Jim. In no way was he to feel any worse than he already did. Of course, he was also the only one to catch any kings, and he caught the first and largest fish, too. In fact, I almost would have liked to be in his boots then … but not later. Nick caught the biggest rainbow and mine was quite a bit smaller. Who can complain? So, the trip was not a flop for our Lower 48 visitors. They caught the biggest fish on the trip. It's fitting. And, even though I may have written some not-so-nice things about Jim's disaster, if it weren't for him, we *all* would have been cooking salted pants and socks.

Grandpa was trying to get me girls during the whole trip. He had lots of great insight and had all the tricks of the trade mastered. Unfortunately, I couldn't really use any of it on this trip, but I will take the secrets with me into the coming years. I'm glad Jim, Nick, Grandpa and Grandma could make it up here, and I hope they'll feel free to come up again. (I've been to Wisconsin to see them hundreds of times.) See you later, Bill

Jim writes: Hi to all. Plattville, Wisconsin is much removed from the location of our trip so I will need to use our pictures from the trip; not to help me remember, but rather to keep things in order. It is hard to keep things and events in sequence because we were so busy. But first things first. This is my first attempt at a letter like this and, as you can see, I tend to write in one long sentence so bear with me, please.

Anyways, Dad, Bill, Nick and I would have not been able to go on this trip without the help of my brother. Thanks! The organizing, calling, gathering equipment must have been challenging.

This brings me to one recurring thought—how much I had to learn or understand! So many times Bill had to explain things to me first, then follow that step by driving the new thought process into my head. The trip was first planned around the July 4 holiday. This seemed logical to me because we would gain an extra day from the holiday. Right? It took several calls and letters before my brother got through to me. No matter how many days we would gain over the holiday—that is when the salmon runs are their lowest. "There ain't no fish in the rivers, Jim, and the tides will be at their worst!" You know, simple things like that are hard for a guy in Wisconsin to understand but I'm starting to get the hang of it.

Our first night in Anchorage, I relearned the sun-up–sun-down theory, Alaska style. Nick and I slept that night in the camper in the driveway in front of Karel and Bill's house. At 12:30 a.m. I was taking pictures of their house and I had to close the blinds to make the camper dark enough. Finally, after a week of camping, I found my flashlight. I didn't use it once all week!

As my pictures remind me, we didn't have to travel very far to see Dall sheep, eagles, and moose. Portage Lake was filled with baby icebergs that had fallen from the glacier. This was a tremendous backdrop for the first of many group photos. The scenery was just wonderful.

Our first camp was at the mouth of Deep Creek. Our site was a short walking distance from a beach of Cook Inlet. I think this campground can best be described as a gravel parking lot with oversized parking spaces. As I think about it, it was set up as a place to park big recreational vehicles with a place for their fishing boat. This was a noisy place with activity all night long.

We had only a short walk to our first fishing spot on Deep Creek where we landed my first king salmon, estimated at 30 pounds. What a beautiful fish! It was then that I learned that you don't just catch them, you have to kill them! What excitement!

Eagles flying overhead and the view of the mountains across the inlet were tremendous. I tried to take a picture—at 12:30 a.m.!—with the sun setting behind the mountain but it just didn't do it justice. Very few of the *big* pictures I took really *worked*. I think I could have fished that spot for the rest of the trip.

At about this point, my memory becomes foggy. That first fishing outing started around 5:45 a.m. and we alternated between sleeping, eating, and fishing from this point on and did little sleeping and eating! We, Nick, Bill Jr. and I, did catch another king at Deep Creek, approximately 20 pounds, but I'll let Nick write about that fish and our mini adventure.

We moved our camp to the Ninilchik River Campground. This was much more your traditional campsite with a place to pitch the tent. While we were there, my mother and Karel stopped for a visit. My brother fixed a tremendous meal of salmon fillet and caribou on the grill. What a meal. When we ate, we ate well! Usually our meals got moved to unusual times because fishing was more important. Nick, Bill Jr., and Dad elected to carry food with them because they were never sure what time they would eat next. It all blurred together there for a while.

We had planned to go onto Cook Inlet to troll for kings with Bill's friend, Nick, but we had to cancel because of bad weather. Then, high winds kept us off the inlet for two more days. These would have been great chances for salmon and halibut … but … as my son says, "That's fishing, Dad."

From our Ninilchik camp site, we could walk to the river and I learned the frustration of being able to see fish, but not being able to hook any. From there we moved our camp to a pretty site right on Skilak Lake so we could be closer to the Kenai River and a quick fishing trip on the Russian River.

This last move set us up for our float trip on the Kenai River. What a day and what a place to fish —and again my pictures did not do it justice. The drift boats were cool. The guides put us on huge pools that looked like they would be full of fish. These sights kept me fascinated and Nick had to bring it to my attention that I didn't catch any fish. After I thought about it, I had to admit that he was right!

One of my last personal discoveries came during the drive back to Anchorage. After a week of tremendous scenery and having eagles flying overhead I began to notice things that I hadn't seen before, like power lines going up a hillside and the smashed grass and brush left by last winter. I realized that these things offended me and I asked myself, why did they have to do that? Earlier in the trip, I hadn't even noticed these kinds of things.

Spending this time with my family was great!

More next year,

Jim

Nick writes: Well, to begin with, I would like to thank everyone who made this trip possible. This includes Uncle Bill, his friends, Dad, Grandpa, and many others. This trip began as a brainchild of my Dad's and is one of the few that has turned out for the better. I would say that all the planning and preparation they put into it was what made this trip a success.

Dad and I started out for the airport with high hopes and prayers for good weather. Our prayers were answered because the weather was very good except for some wind out on the ocean, but that didn't stop us, only our captain.

The trip started out excellent. Dad caught and landed his first king, with little or no trouble. Then after talking to Uncle Bill's friend Nick, a great guy with a great name, we decided against going trolling for what he called feeder kings. He did give us detailed advice on where and how to fish Deep Creek though, so we set out.

Nick had positioned Dad, Bill Jr., and me on a small island where we could fish the incoming tide. After a brief time of casting and changing lures, Dad tied into one of the huge fish. He had already caught one and he handed the rod to me. I fought the fish for a good seven minutes. Soon I was very tired, so I passed the rod to Bill Jr. He quickly led the fish into the net I was holding. Bill and I went back to fishing because we figured "Hey, It's just starting," but Dad went and walked around the island for a bit. The next thing we knew, he was telling us to pick up our stuff and get out of there. Now!

The tide was coming in and soon our little island would be covered by water. Dad had visions of people finding our bones there, so he decided that he was getting off the island right then, and nothing was going to stand in his way. To Bill's and my dismay, Dad walked right off the island into the deepest water. It went over his hip boots by a good six inches. Thanks to Dad, Bill and I knew where the deep water was, so we slowly inched our way through the shallows across the river. Bill and I made it across the river dry, so we started to fish again, but Dad wasn't so lucky. He sat down and tried to dry out the best he could. That night Dad cooked his socks over the campfire. It still makes me laugh just thinking about it.

Jim stepped in a deep hole and proved why the stream was named Deep Creek, now he is drying his socks.

One of the things I couldn't get over was the incredible scenery. It seemed as if we couldn't get away from it. One thing is for sure. Alaska looks a lot different from Wisconsin. Dad and I went from looking at cornfields to mountains and glaciers.

This was a trip for all ages. A Dad with his two sons who were with their sons. I think and hope that this can become a Hauser family tradition. I would like to give everyone one last "Thank you" because I had the best time of my life on this trip.

Nick Hauser

P.S. This was the second edition of this letter. Just as I was about to print the first copy my computer crashed. I had to retype it all again.

Grandpa (Bill) Hauser writes:

August 1

This is about a fishing trip to Alaska in June of 1994 when Grandma and I took a two-week vacation. My son, Jim, and his son, Nick, met us in Anchorage for one week of fishing and camping.

The week ended up as a fishing trip with my two sons and their two sons which made grandpa one proud monarch.

My son, Bill, had everything planned and scheduled, such as time of day, place, kind of fish, plus food. Nobody has ever seen two teenagers, Bill G. and Nick, eat so many pretzels in one week. A four-pound bag as big as three loaves of bread, GORP, M & Ms, raisins, you name it, soda pop, and more. Plus regular meals.

When Bill retires I can see him as an outfitter. However, the weather cannot be counted on; you see, we were blown off the ocean for two days. So halibut fishing was canceled. The camp grounds were all very suitable. We also saw some wildlife, including more eagles than I expected. No bear, though.

Now for fishing … did we try? You can imagine five people giving it all they got trying.

Note, one of the pictures taken shows me sitting in the boat in hip boots and full dress *watching*. That's my strong point; however, I found fish in Alaska is no guarantee.

At this time it would be impossible to detail each day, but everything worked A-okay. And all had a good time.

The Ford Explorer towed the trailer very good and also got good gas mileage.

We returned on a Friday and unpacked. Jim and Nick returned to the Lower 48 on Friday evening and back to work on Monday. Grandma and I returned on Wednesday. One thing I found annoying was time change and jet lag.

I must thank Bill for all the work, though, and the organizing he did for us.

I also wish to thank Jim, Nick, and Bill G. for babysitting Grandpa.

I don't think anybody can understand how proud I am that I could be with my two sons, Bill and Jim, and their two sons, Bill and Nick. I would not have missed this for anything in the world.

Grandpa Bill Hauser

August 20

I have thought many times about an ending for this letter. Now I am ready to end it and I cannot think. The trip was wonderful. I have thought about it again and again. And I have enjoyed the thoughts of the others you have just read.

Dad was just great. He warned us that he might have some trouble getting around. He was involved in everything! He was a little slow, but he seemed to get stronger daily. He never held back. He fished as hard as anyone! We all had fun and we all had fun together.

And, together, we exploded the great Alaska myth! The fish do not simply leap into your net. Sometimes, they do not even get on your hook. We found fish, we could see them. But they just would not bite. Nevertheless, the comradeship was great. We all learned new things and we all shared. I am ready to do it all over again but it cannot be duplicated. This had to be the true fishing and camping trip of a lifetime ... with a Dad and his sons and their sons. I was so lucky to be a part of it and to be able to help it happen. I am very proud of my family.

Now this must end. This letter may be a bit long, but it is a special record of a special event.

Bye for now,

Love,

Bill, Bill, Bill, Jim and Nick

October 17, 2008

Oh, wait, there is more ... Did you notice that my Dad, Jim, and Nick all commented about all the bald eagles they saw? We, in Alaska, almost take them for granted. We always appreciate them and share a sighting with each other just as we do for any wildlife sighting. But it is easy for us to forget that it is different for visitors from Outside. For them, a sighting of our national emblem is a rare event.

There are not many in the immediate Anchorage area, but they do fly over our house several times each year. They are much more common just east of Anchorage, along Turnagain Arm, especially when fish are migrating through.

During the 1900s, the bald eagle nearly became extinct in the Lower 48, but not in Alaska. Now, of course, they have been removed from the endangered listing and are becoming more abundant. I am aware, for example, that they have become quite common along the Mississippi and Wisconsin Rivers where they have a good source of their favorite food—fish. They do eat other things, of course, like small mammals, birds, and carrion.

Considering that bald eagles are fish-eating birds and Alaska has a fishing culture, you can bet that the relationship was not always rosy. Fishermen claimed that bald eagles were the cause for a decline of salmon and convinced the Territorial Legislature in 1917 to impose a bounty of $2 for a pair of eagle feet. Over 100,000 eagles were killed before the bounty was eliminated in 1953, six years before statehood. Today, there are an estimated 70,000 to 100, 000 bald eagles in the world and roughly half are found in Alaska. They are frequently sighted in coastal areas and around big rivers and lakes.

Bald eagles do not mature until they are about age five. As juveniles, they are rather nondescript with a streaked dark brown coloration. Their bright white head and tail feathers are a mark of maturity. They mate for life and like to nest in tall sturdy trees. They use and rebuild nests for many years and the nests can become quite large—12 to 20 feet high and 8 to 10 feet across. Occasionally, they become so large and heavy that they crash to the ground. Eagle nest trees are now protected by federal regulation.

The world's greatest concentration of bald eagles happens each winter in the 48,000-acre Chilkat Bald Eagle Preserve near Haines. Between October and December, some 3,000 to 5,000 bald eagles, along with thousands of golden eagles congregate on the Chilkat River flats. Of these, only between 200 and 400 are residents. The eagles gather here because of an interesting convergence of river hydrology, fish biology, and eagle ecology. This area of the river has many upwelling, or spring-like, areas. During fall and winter, the upwelling river water is warmer than surface runoff water, so there is a five-mile reach that is mainly ice free. Salmon, especially chum salmon, like to spawn in upwelling water areas. Because the water is relatively warm, the salmon eggs hatch in fewer days than usual, so the adult salmon spawn later in the year than most other populations. Eagles like to eat fish and this is their last, best chance to gorge on a concentration of energy-rich salmon until after the winter has ended. So they flock in from many miles away.

Historically, Alaskans have had had a love-hate relationship with eagles, but I can assure you that we appreciate eagles as much as you do. We are just fortunate enough to see them more often than you may.

One last tidbit. Golden eagles are also found in Alaska but they are found in more northerly inland areas and prefer more rocky and drier terrain. They feed mainly on small mammals, birds, and carrion.

Link: American Bald Eagle Information
http://www.baldeagleinfo.com/

Chapter Ten
Chignik

More than a place. An experience.

September 3, 2007

Hey. Hello. How are you today?

I certainly hope that you are having a great summer and that all is well with you and your family.

I am feeling good and getting ready to leave on a trip, but first, I do want to tell you about the trip that I returned from just a week ago.

It was a great trip and, as it happened, it was through this trip that I discovered a new special cap. We all have some special mug or tee shirt or cap which evokes some special memory, right? As I packed for the trip, I knew I would need a cap. But which one? I own about a dozen. One cap was too warm; another too cool. One seemed too new and too clean and without any special history. But, finally, I chose that one for the weeklong trip and I was on my way to Chignik.

Chignik—which means "big wind"—is on the Alaska Peninsula, west from the south end of Kodiak Island and across Shelikof Strait. It is about 450 miles southwest of Anchorage. Chignik is actually many things. Chignik is a lake and a river and a village and, in particular, it is a special place where Peter, my son-in-law, has been working for three years on a research project for his master's degree in fisheries from the University of Washington. His project is in Chignik because the entire drainage comprises a highly productive salmon system. He has completed the requirements for the degree, but he returned to Chignik on one last trip to help to close down and winterize the University of Washington Fisheries Research Institute (FRI) research camp. For a birthday present, my family arranged for me to come along to help. Peter especially wanted to share this "magical"—his description—bit of Alaska with me. It turned out to be a very special and amazing birthday present.

A typical scene at Chignik includes black volcanic sand, mountains, and clouds but it often includes rain and wind, too.

We flew to the village of King Salmon, transferred to a smaller plane, and continued to Chignik Village. Our scheduled boat ride across Chignik Lake to the FRI camp was unexpectedly absent, but Peter quickly arranged an alternate. We dropped our duffel at the camp and took a short skiff ride down the Chignik River to visit the Alaska Department of Fish and Game crew at their huge fish-counting weir. This weir is an important tool to evaluate the run strength of Chinook, sockeye, coho, and pink salmon that return to the Chignik system and Peter wanted to get the most recent update. Fresh Chinook and sockeye were still entering the system and the coho run was just getting underway. We returned to camp and caught Dolly Varden until Ryan and Ben returned from their sampling trip from upriver.

We ate a late supper as Peter, Ryan, and Ben brought each other up on the ongoing research and work that was done or still needed to be done. From this point on, the days became a blur. Some days, we slept in and some days we started early. Some activities were leisurely, some, intense. Some activities were scheduled according to tidal movements. The days were shortening, but it was still light until late in the evening. There was no predictable schedule and it was hard to keep track of time. During the week I was at Chignik, we were able to enjoy ample time for fishing, but after I left, two more workers arrived for the final frantic week of hard work.

I fished at least once every day, mostly, for Dolly Varden. They came in all sizes, up to 28 inches. Dollies spawn in the fall and their bright, almost gaudy colors were just beginning to develop. One day, the four of us met with two other friends and fished a tributary to Chignik Lake where we found a dense school of Dollies concentrated in one pool of a small stream. But they would not cooperate. We explored other parts of the stream and we tried different lures and flies as our effort shrank to six anglers casting toward this one school of fish in this one pool. Someone switched from a large- to a small-sized salmon egg imitation and suddenly, a fish! Another! After a third fish, there were six believers. The small egg imitations were shared and the fly rod passed from one person to another. More egg imitations were shared. It was great fun! It was like six little kids around one little pond. And we were again impressed with the simple rule of fishing. Right time, right place, right bait.

Another day, Peter, Ben, and I took the skiff with a jet unit on the outboard and went upriver through the length of Chignik Lake and Black River, into Black Lake and up a tributary stream. The trip alone was like an adventure. The Chignik drainage straddles the Alaska Peninsula. Chignik Lake is on the Gulf of Alaska side. Black Lake is on the Bering Sea side. The Black River is a thin corridor through the Alaska Mountain Range that forms the backbone of the peninsula. As we scooted up the river and through the opening of the mountain range, the active volcano, Mount Veniemenoff, showed itself from the south. This is a broad, snow-covered peak, but it was still impressive as the snow glowed in the blast of sunlight that broke through the clouds. We tried to pick our way through the shallow braids of the river delta but we did need to jump out a couple times to pull and push the shallow draft boat into a channel which was deep enough to run the jet unit. Fortunately, most of the substrate is black volcanic sand instead of rocks.

At Chignik, bears were never far away

We were richly rewarded for those efforts. The river was home for the early run of sockeye salmon and the stream was filled with the bright red and green spawning fish that rested in the pools and splashed in the riffles. Dolly Varden filled the stream, too. They were there to feed voraciously on salmon eggs that were not properly buried and on the bits of flesh from the decomposing carcasses. And, the sockeye salmon were easy prey for the bears. No black bears here; only grizzly. They had trampled the bank vegetation flat. Fish heads and half-eaten carcasses littered the sandy beaches. We saw about 10, perhaps 15 bears as we ran upriver about seven miles and about the same number when we returned downstream. Many turned and ran as soon as they heard us approach, but others stood on their hind legs for a better look before they dissolved into the bushes.

The Dolly fishing was fast. Ben and I focused mainly on a deep pool that held numerous resting fish. We simply cast out and took whatever bit—potluck. Peter took advantage of the clear, shallow water to seek out individual fish and cast directly to them. I caught and measured one Dolly at 24 inches. Peter's largest was 28 inches.

The North Pacific Ocean crashes against tall dramatic cliffs of the Alaska Peninsula. The formation known as Caste Cape is in the background.

Peter also arranged with a friend, John, to take us for a day on his 42-foot seine boat. John has worked and fished the Chignik area for over 20 years and he now operates a guiding service for salmon, Dollies, and saltwater fish (Chignik Bay Alaska Adventures charter and guide service). From the FRI camp, we took the skiff to run down the Chignik River, through the gate in the Fish and Game weir, through Chignik Lagoon and around to the village of Chignik Bay. John took us out of Chignik Bay and into the north Gulf of Alaska, southwest along the south edge of the Alaska Peninsula. The scenery alone was worth the effort. Thousand-foot cliffs rose vertically from the water. One formation, with four tall spires, was aptly named Castle Point. Puffins and sea otters were all about, along with other seabirds. Eagles. Harbor seals. As we ran to and from Chignik Bay, we had a humpback whale spout within 100 yards and we apparently surprised one sea otter which popped up at about 20 feet off the bow. It took one glimpse before it dived.

We all passed on going shark fishing but preferred a greater variety of smaller fish. We caught—mostly with fly rods—black rockfish, greenlings, halibut, and others. It was too early for fly-fishing for coho, but we tried anyway. It was a gas!

John was able to tease the rockfish up near to the rail of the boat. We could see them take a fly and several were caught by pulling the fly along the surface. Halibut were encouraged by chumming and we were encouraged by the shallow water. A mere 30 feet. One fly-caught halibut was about 15 to 20 pounds. Later we pulled a couple crab pots. Supper consisted of a meal of beer-battered halibut and rockfish and steamed tanner crab … all caught less than four hours earlier.

Black rockfish have a general resemblance to freshwater black bass. They are not usually caught by fly fishing.

We even did some work. We clipped and saved a small piece of the tail fin from the Dolly Varden we caught from the Black Lake tributary. These were labeled and preserved for genetic analysis as part of a study to determine the number of spawning stocks in the Chignik drainage. One day, we used a beach seine to collect fish from five sites around Chignik Lagoon. The fish collections focused on juvenile sockeye salmon. This research project and other studies, including genetic analysis, would be used to determine the spawning stocks which contributed to the Chignik Lagoon rearing populations.

You see, Chignik Drainage is a particularly interesting place for a fish biologist. This small system produces goodly numbers of sockeye, Chinook, and coho salmon, as well as pink salmon during even-numbered years. Sockeye are, perhaps, the most interesting. Sockeye salmon depend on lakes for the young fish to find their favorite foods. Chignik Lake is a fine example of a deep, cold sockeye salmon rearing lake. But you also know that for every rule there is an exception. Actually, there are two exceptions to the rule in the Chignik Drainage. Black Lake is a fine producer of young sockeyes, but it is shallow, weedy, and relatively warm. Numerous young sockeye also rear in Chignik Lagoon where we measured salinities from almost pure freshwater to almost pure saltwater. Early-run sockeyes spawn in the upper tributaries. Late-run sockeyes spawn mainly in the Chignik River. To make it more interesting, the hydrology of the rivers is changing, which probably allows more young sockeyes to move downstream away from rearing areas in Black Lake.

One haul of a beach seine yields a good catch of mixed species to sort, identify, and count.

This leaves fish biologists such as Peter—and me—asking endless "what if" questions and pondering. Where do fry from the different spawning stocks actually rear? Which rearing area is producing the most adults? Do those that rear in the lagoon survive the winter? If yes, where? And where do the adults spawn? What do the fry eat in the different rearing areas? What will be the long-term impact of the changing hydrology at Black Lake? Scientists delight in asking new and intriguing questions.

Peter reveled in the opportunity to do his own research and to live and learn fish biology in the wonderful complexity that is Chignik. And I was so fortunate that he was so willing to show me this special area and exhibit the physical and biological challenges that he studied. Many biologists face challenges as they do their research, but few are fortunate to study their subjects from the very top of a drainage to the very bottom. And I was pleased that Peter cared so much to invite me to experience a small measure of what he has experienced.

Along the way, we had caught fresh and dark sockeye salmon and the delightful Dolly Varden, but we had really been looking forward to catching some coho salmon. These are strong fish and usually quite willing to take a fly. Peter did land a couple, we both had some on, and we had good follows. I had not landed any and although we both knew that the run was just starting, I could sense that Peter was anxious and hopeful that I would catch one.

Here is where this becomes a picture-perfect storybook ending for this trip and this letter.

I was scheduled on a flight from Chignik Village with a departure time of 9 a.m. on Peninsula Airways. The gravel airstrip is about a one-mile boat ride and a five-minute walk from the FRI camp. As I sorted and packed the night before, Peter asked, “You do want to fish once more in the morning before you leave, don’t you?”

“Of course.”

We were on the water, just below the camp, as it was becoming light enough to fish, shortly after seven o’clock. We were casting 4-inch-long pink bunny strip flies and using a stripping retrieve technique. At about 7:30, our handheld radio broadcast that the plane should land in Chignik Village before 8:30 to pick up one passenger. At abut 7:50, I tangled my line and as I cleared the tangle, Peter walked over while he furled his rod and line. I cut off my fly. Peter asked why. I said that I thought we had to go. “Oh, no; there is still plenty of time.”

I retied. I made four, maybe six casts. Across the current. Allow the fly to sink as it swings with the current. Strip it back in foot-long jerks. Just as the swing ended, there was a solid, commanding take! I stripped back hard with my left hand to set the hook! Everything by the book! A happy shout from Peter! The fish sped off downstream! Fast! The handle on the backward-spinning spool thumped my knuckles. The fish slowed briefly, but sped onward again.

Whoa! My 90-foot fly line was off the reel and I was into the backing. The fish was at least 130 feet away. I glanced to the shore because I needed to follow this strong fish. “Uh. Peter, look there.” About 200 feet downstream, a mom grizzly bear and her cub were watching us. Both were up on their hind legs so they could get a better look. Cub in front. Low bushes on one side and the river on the other. Pristine setting. Picture perfect. No camera. We talked to the bears and then we raised our voices a little louder. They turned and disappeared around the corner. Out of sight but not out of mind.

I managed to work the fish and tire it out so I could bring it to us. It was a fine, beautiful, bright male. At least 12 pounds, maybe a bit more. The jaw was beginning to form a hook and it still bore sea lice. Picture perfect. No camera. No problem. We turned it over and admired it. Removed the hook. Held it in the current and watched it swim away.

I clipped off the fly and wound up the line. We turned and headed for the cabin. We arrived just in time to hear the radio crackle again. The plane was on its final approach. We were down the path and into the skiff. Three pulls on the starter rope. Nothing. Two more pulls and we were off. Dash across the lake. Beach the skiff, toss out the anchor. Grab a load. Up the path to the end of the airstrip. Chock the cooler and other gear into the space in the back of the plane. The hatch is closed. "Goodbye and thank you, Peter." Into a seat and the door slams. Fasten seatbelt. The engine starts. We are airborne. It is 8:50 a.m.

It was a special treat to see the confluence of several glaciers from the airplane on the return flight from Chignik.

A wonderful ending to a wonderful week.

Don't you agree that I now have a very special fishing cap that will evoke a flood of fond memories every time I look at it?

Special wishes to you from Alaska.

Love

Bill

August 9, 2008

Oh, wait, there is more ... those rockfish that we were catching near Castle Point outside Chignik Lagoon belong to one species in a large family of mostly marine fishes. Of more than a hundred species of rockfish—genus *Sebastes*—most are found in the North Pacific Ocean and more than 30 species are in Alaska waters.

Rockfish have strong spines in their fins and around their heads. In general appearance, they resemble the widespread freshwater black bass which are not closely related; hence, dark-skinned rockfish are often called black bass or sea bass.

Most rockfish live near the bottom, often around rocky areas. Some species inhabit shallow water and others deeper water to over a 1,000 feet deep. A few species are free-swimming and are often found close to the surface. Typically, rockfish do not travel far from a preferred location.

Adults of some species of Alaska rockfish grow to about 5 inches; others may be up to about 40 inches.

There are two particularly interesting facts about rockfishes. One, most live to a very old age. Two, they give birth to live young.

Rockfish grow slowly, but they live long; therefore, any big rockfish is old, very old. Shortraker rockfish which is found in deep water in the North Pacific, as an example, may grow to about three feet long and weigh about 40 pounds, but it takes about 90 to 115 years. A rougheye rockfish caught in Alaska waters was at least 170 years old and as much as 205 years, the oldest of any known fish of any species. That fish could have been alive while Lewis and Clark were trekking across the western United States. Exact age is very difficult to determine because the slow rate of growth causes tightly spaced growth rings that are challenging to distinguish.

As it happens, the rockfish we were catching on flies were one of, if not the fastest growing rockfish. They reach maturity at approximately 10 years in Alaska waters and years earlier in southern parts of the rang. They are much more productive than other species and therefore, less vulnerable to overfishing.

Rockfish have internal fertilization and the eggs develop within the ovary of the female. Live birth happens shortly after the larvae hatch. Large numbers of feeble-swimming young are produced. Live birth is not highly unusual among fish species but it is the exception to the rule. Sexual maturity occurs late in life among most rockfishes, usually after age 10 or 15.

Rockfish are flavorful and pursued by sport and commercial fishermen which puts them in a hazardous situation. Because they grow slowly, live to an old age, and require a number of years before maturity, they are particularly vulnerable to overfishing. In addition, rockfishes have a gas bladder so they can adjust their buoyancy at different depths. When they are brought quickly to the surface, the gas expands with the loss of water pressure and the bladder expands. If they are returned to the water, they cannot dive and most will perish.

One last tidbit. All rockfishes are marine, but another genus in the family, sculpins, includes some freshwater species.

Link: for a wide variety of information about rockfishes use Google to search the web–enter rockfish or Sebastes with another word such as age, growth, or reproduction

Section Three—Hunt Alaska

Chapter Eleven
My First Sheep Hunting Trip, An Instant Success

When I was young, I read about hunting Dall sheep in sporting magazines, but I never dreamed that I would make such a hunt. I made my rookie sheep hunt during my third year in Alaska.

September 2, 1983

Well, good morning.

Let's see. Where to start? Ah! Coffee. I have worked and puttered to get my one-burner stove going and I put about two cups of water in a pot. Now it's boiling already. Break time!

Okay, I have my coffee and I've started more water to boil. Soon, I'll have my breakfast of instant oatmeal and I'll have more hot water waiting for my partner, Phil, when he gets up. He is still in his sack in our tent. I'm sitting in a dismal little well-used 8-by-12-foot shack. We should be out sheep hunting, but we're weathered in today or, weathered out of the mountains. It rained most of last night and turned to light snow this morning. We had to get up at midnight to put a waterproof cover over our caribou meat so it wouldn't get wet.

Phil is up and the water's not hot yet. Too bad! Anyhow, since we can't hunt, we have all day to sit around and this epistle may be long. I guess that's all right because I owe so many of you a letter or two.

The sun! It showed bright through the overcast and the wind but it did not last long. The sun is gone already. But I've had my oatmeal and checked the meat and brushed my teeth and now, I've got my second cup of coffee.

Anyhow, I hope you don't mind these occasional photocopied letters. I guess I rather enjoy writing them and sharing my experiences with you, but I just can't write a separate letter to each of you, even though I'd like to.

I guess that if Phil and I were truly master sheep hunters we'd be on our way up the side of a mountain right now. I guess we are not. And I guess we've both lost a lot of our optimism. Besides, Phil's boots are wet. Soaked, from crossing the creek about ten times yesterday and he lost his feet, too.

We flew into this remote airstrip adjacent to Baultoff Creek at 4,000-feet elevation near Northway, Alaska. We're five miles from the Canadian border. We came in on August 27. We stashed part of our gear close to this cabin and packed our spike camp about four miles up the creek where we hunted for two days. Gorgeous country! The first day we were excited to see about a hundred sheep and finally located two legal rams. We had to backtrack down the mountain, around, and back up to get to them. By then they had vanished! Chalk that up to experience!

Miners who worked the Baultoff Creek drainage near Northway, built and later abandoned this little shack near the airstrip. It could barely accommodate two people but it was handy when we were in camp and the weather was bad.

We hunted another day and enjoyed being in high country, but we saw no rams. That evening we moved our camp back down to the airstrip. The next day, we got up into more high country where we saw more sheep; some closer than ever, including several sublegal rams. This day, Phil lost his feet.

He had had a few blisters, which he took care of, but finally he could not walk without pain when we were still about two and a half hours away from camp. It actually took us about four hours to get back.

Yesterday, September 1, the caribou season opened. We had seen some in this vicinity almost daily. We had seen at least three especially nice bulls and a few cows. Yesterday was our day to get a caribou. We started at 6 a.m. and we were finished hunting in two hours.

Phil had worked east from the airstrip, I, west. I got mine first. Phil reacted

It is always exhilarating to be in the high country, especially with bright, fresh snow and tundra in fall colors.

Dall sheep habitat merges with caribou habitat in the lower valleys.

by coming toward the shots when he spotted three caribou close by our camp. Probably, these were from the same group of four that I had found. He said that he ran down through the timber, across the tundra, past the willows, and across the stream to head them off before they moved too far. By the time he got close enough to shoot, he was too tired and had trouble shooting, but he did hit the biggest of the three. Unfortunately, it had already crossed the main stem of Baultoff Creek. Phil saw it disappear in the brush on the other side and took off after it. Unfortunately, his route took him right through a deep pool so he got soaked to the knees. "There was water flying and grayling jumping everywhere!" he said.

He got a nice bull. And it was only about 400 yards from camp, so he had a nice easy pack to get the meat to camp. Unfortunately, he had to cross Baultoff Creak each time. He had to make at least four round trips to get it all hauled out.

I'm sure glad I shot mine early in the day. I spent all day getting it cleaned, skinned, and butchered. The rack from mine is almost 3 feet high and 2 ½ feet wide. Nice, but not real big. The rack from Phil's bull is wider and it has double shovels; mine is higher and has more points.

Sometimes, if you stare hard enough and long enough at one of those little white dots, it becomes a sheep.

Anyhow, I was very careful not to waste meat or get hair on it. Finally, it took me four round trips to get it all back to camp. About sixty or more pounds per trip. It's all boned except the legs. I have, I think, nearly 200 pounds of meat. It was about a three-fourths-mile pack; but it was an easy pack, downhill, along a trail and one step across creek. Forty-five minutes for a round trip.

Boy, I couldn't even turn the carcass over by myself! I could move it a bit, though. Phil's was on a slope and, when it fell, it wrapped itself around a tree. I guess he really had a fun time.

September 3

This day was a good day and a bad day. We were up at 5 a.m. as usual and off. Early on, we spotted a nice sheep, but it was too far off to tell if it was legal-sized.

Time out for supper—it's already cooked. With freeze-dried foods, all you need to do is boil water, add it to the food pouch and allow it to reconstitute for 10 minutes. Done. No challenge, no problem.

September 4

Good morning. Again.

According to the clock, we should be halfway back to Northway by now. We're ready to go, but we need a plane first. With a pilot. Unfortunately, I don't think the pilot will bring his plane here for a while. You're right. I'm weathered in. Unfortunately, today …

Hey! We made it out! We sure didn't expect to see that plane today! But we were ready anyhow. Now, we're in the Northway Lodge waiting for the pilot to get back with his second trip so we can get on the road back to Anchorage. He has to pick up and bring out another party from some other location. Along the way, he will stop for the two front shoulders from my caribou, too. If he had known how heavy the load actually was, he probably would have left even more for the second load. As it was, I said a little prayer as we bounced down the gravel airstrip. It felt as if we just made it airborne!

I just called Karel. I will see her and the kids in 10 or 12 hours.

Altogether, we saw about 200 sheep. Many, of course, we probably saw several times. We saw about 20 mature rams. Of these, five were legal. Of these, three were full-curls. Of these, two were magnificent!

Yesterday. What a sight! Five rams standing together. Right on the skyline! What a marvelous way to end the hunt.

September 6

Back to reality. I'm eating my lunch at work. I haven't heard so many moose-, sheep-, caribou-, and duck-hunting stories for a long time! One guy upstairs got a nice bull moose right off the main highway before he even got to his hunting camp.

Actually, I should be out running (I forgot to bring my towel). I've jogged regularly since January and I plan to keep it up for another 40 or 50 years. It sure makes a difference. I sure felt good. I lost 4 pounds last week, too.

I'll tell you what; if you want to come hunting in Alaska, plan ahead, get in good shape, and get some good boots.

Our last day of hunting was exciting. We tried to slip up to some rams, which eluded us when suddenly, we saw them standing, shoulder to shoulder, looking down on us from the skyline with utter disdain. Three were full-curl; two of these were magnificent. It was a most fantastic sight that I will never forget. (I can still see a mental image of this sight as I review this letter, 26 years later.)

The bad part of it was that we wanted a ram so badly that after we had worked as close as possible, we took several shots. The distance was, however, still too far for a well-placed shot and we were embarrassed at this. Fortunately, we followed up and were relieved to learn that none was wounded and escaped.

Most of the caribou meat has been taken care of. It tastes great! We'll have hamburger, salami, polish sausage made. Now I'd like to fill out the freezer with a few more salmon and maybe some ducks and a few ptarmigan.

Anyhow, we had a great hunt and a fantastic week. We were not lucky enough to get a sheep, but to just be out in sheep country and enjoy those wonderful, panoramic views was a reward in itself. And besides, the caribou hunt was a success in itself.

Now, it feels good to be home again with my family.

Love to all of you. Hope this hasn't bored you.

Bill

P.S. Maybe you are all glad that I get weathered in occasionally; otherwise you'd not get any letters from me.

February 20, 2007

Oh, wait, there is another thing … Dall sheep are beautiful animals that many hunters regard as an elegant and challenging trophy. Here in Alaska, we are fortunate that Dall sheep are found in many mountain ranges. They are mostly found above the timberline in the highest parts of the mountains and on some of the steeper alpine slopes. They are rarely far from rugged areas that can provide refuge from predators.

Dall sheep have a white coat with curling brownish-yellow horns. Horns grow continuously and are not shed; antlers are grown and shed annually. Both male, called rams, and female, called ewes, Dall sheep have horns. The horns of ewe and juvenile males, however, are much smaller and less curved than the mature males. Horns of males grow in a circular pattern throughout their lives and a ram with a complete circle or full curl, is usually about 7 years old. Rams with horns larger than full curl are uncommon, but are truly impressive. Males develop a system of social hierarchy based on horn size and the horns are used for jousting and clashing, especially during the rutting season.

Ewes move to rugged areas in late spring for lambing but the lambs are soon able to negotiate the steep terrain and begin to feed on vegetation. By midsummer, the ewes and lambs merge into flocks of a half dozen or so to as many as 30 or 40. Mature males are more solitary, but may be in groups of about three to six.

Summertime food is abundant and consists of a variety of

vegetation such as grasses, sedges, and leafy plants. Good nutrition is important during the summer because winter is a time of scarcity. Food is harder to find and it is mainly found in areas that are blown free of snow by the wind. Horn growth is slower in winter because there is a striking difference in food intake during the different seasons; consequently, annual marks are discernable on the horns and the age of the animals can be determined. When conditions are good, herd sizes expand, but a year or two of bad winter weather can trim the herd size.

The hunting season for Dall sheep traditionally begins on August 10 each year, but good planning is required if you are interested in pursuing one of these trophies. Much of the available territory has hunting allowed by lottery drawing permit only and the application period is November 1 through December 6 for the following summer. In addition, nonresident hunters are required to hunt with a guide. Further, Dall sheep are commonly found in more inaccessible parts of the state so a hunter will usually need to make arrangements for transportation by light aircraft into the hunting zone. Sometimes, Dall sheep are accessible from the road system, but every sheep hunt will ultimately depend on walking in rugged terrain ... with your food and your camp on your back. You will need to be in good physical condition and you will need good, lightweight, reliable equipment.

One last tidbit ... If you decide to photograph or hunt for Dall sheep, I hope you will have a great experience, but above all, do enjoy the spectacular scenery and the sheer pleasure of being in such a wonderful setting.

Link: Alaska Department of Fish and Game
http://www.adfg.state.ak.us/
ADF&G Wildlife Notebook Series
http://www.adfg.state.ak.us/pubs/notebook/notehome.php

Chapter Twelve
A Near Disaster

We ended this sheep hunt without even hunting.

August 27, 1984

Hello.

Wow, this is the first time in three days that I've had any chance to relax. I am on my annual sheep hunt. Actually, close to the end of this trip, I hope, even though this trip was scheduled for six days of sheep hunting and three days of caribou hunting. Now, we only want it to end. And we haven't even actually tried to hunt sheep.

My partner, Phil, and I are ready to get out of here now and just happy to be alive. We've been lucky.

We flew in from Northway on Saturday, August 25. The weather seemed to be improving and clearing. The mosquitoes and black flies were truly troublesome. We backpacked in to a spike camp in about 2 hours. Tee-shirt weather. We had a bit of discussion before we finally selected a barely adequate tent site to make the best of where we were when we stopped hiking. It seemed exposed, but it was the best of the choices even though we had to walk downhill to the stream to get water.

I haven't made much progress here … I'm now in my sleeping bag and looking forward to my first real night's sleep in days. But first, I'm trying to get my toes warmed up.

Let's see … oh. As we set up camp, we began to notice that the wind was picking up and the clouds had become terribly shifty. The squirrelly winds began to spit sleet. Then, it began to snow as we finished our hot supper. Our last hot meal until tonight.

It is still snowing. It has been snowing continuously for 48 hours! The wind has been blowing continuously even longer.

All the while, until 9:15 this morning, we lay in our tent and waited and hoped that the weather would subside.

Once, we had to go outside for a little relief. We planned ahead and did what we had to do in about 15 minutes. We were nearly knocked over by the wind gusts. It was blowing probably about 35 to 50 knots. It was overwhelming. But we had to get out for a quick break and to grab some food. Just some GORP and some jerky. We couldn't find our food bags or our one-burner mountain stove which we had stashed in the lee of a rise under some willows. By that time, the willows were embedded in about 3 feet of drifted snow.

So we spent all the rest of the time in our sleeping bags, waiting. Just waiting for the weather to clear. All the while, the snow filtered down into the tent through the now non-useful mosquito netting. The snow settled into and onto everything. We had cold trail food, but no water.

The mountains are beautiful with a layer of fresh snow but that is where we were supposed to be hunting Dall sheep.

This morning we decided to go for it. I'm surely glad we did. It was a hard trip. It took us 4 hours to walk downhill to the airstrip along the same route that had taken us 2 hours going in, uphill.

The winds had lulled somewhat and it was not too cold. But the snow was very deep in most places. Mostly, we could walk in the creek bottom where it was usually windswept. On level ground, in brushy areas, the snow was knee-deep. But we had to cross many drifts. Most were not more than hip-deep but we did cross one drift which was at least 6 feet deep and 12 feet across. I was thankful that Phil happened to be in the lead at that time.

The bad part is that to keep our pack loads to a minimum we left the tent, which weighed only 3½ pounds. But filled with snow and ice, it probably weighed 10 to 15 pounds. We left some clothes and our food and stove which was now buried under a 5-foot drift.

We were so relieved to get back to the airstrip where we had cached another backup camp. If the weather is better tomorrow, the pilot will be here to check on us, as we had scheduled. Then it will be over. Right now, it would be ludicrous to try to find a sheep. And it would be a horrendous job to try to retrieve our gear. If it rains for a day or two and we are still here, maybe we can look for sheep and get our gear. And maybe a caribou, too.

Good night for now. My feet are finally warm enough so I can fall asleep.

The airstrip was covered with about eight inches of snow. Our sheep hunt was finished before it began.

August 28

Good Morning. Well, actually, it is about noon. I slept in. I got nearly 10 hours of sleep. It was restful. The howling wind abated. A few pings of snowflakes are still hitting our tent but it has nearly stopped snowing now. After 60 or more hours of continuous snowfall. Here, at about 4,000 feet elevation, there is only a foot of accumulation.

We are, of course, feeling much better and the weather is starting to break. We'll talk with the pilot when he comes. If there is an excellent chance of continuous good weather, we may stay. Right now, the air temperature is hovering at the freezing point and the breeze is light. With a good day of thaw, it won't be so hard to get around; with two days, we might be able to go back and retrieve the rest of our gear. It is hard to comprehend that with this storm came the first killing frost. The aspen leaves have not yet turned yellow. It would surely be nice to take home at least a caribou.

I had some coffee earlier and made some improvements to a sort of a lean-to which is beside our tent … Or, maybe our tent is beside the lean-to. Recall that last year on my hunt we stayed near a dismal little shack. Well, it is still here and we are taking advantage of it for some extra shelter and we set up our base camp tent in the lee of the wind.

As it happens, the shack has been blown off the foundation. It is lying on its side beside the floor, which remained attached to the ground. Yesterday, we did some major renovation work on it. We salvaged the woodstove and some stovepipe and, with sheets and pieces of plywood, we expanded one wall and made a corner. We got a small fire started. It felt so good to be warm and we did some drying out. This morning, I tried to plug some more of the holes where the wind came in and the heat went out and I hung a reflective space blanket to lower the ceiling and conserve the heat.

The old shack had been blown off its foundation but the floor made a nice platform for our base camp tent.

Now I'm relaxing in my sleeping bag again and conserving even more heat. Enough for now. Time for some reading.

3:30 p.m.

Oh no! We are still in a state of shock! We just made the most stupid and annoying blunder we could possibly have made. We blew our ride home! We mistakenly waved off the pilot. He didn't even land! We had prearranged signals to alert him to an emergency. Well, we are not in an emergency situation. At least not now. So we did not have our emergency signals out. So as Phil waved his arms and I ran for my signal and pointed down; the pilot wagged the plane; which means: received and understood your message. Unfortunately, he got the wrong message. Then he kept on flying until the sound of the engine dissolved from the valley.

I'll tell you what! My partner is a nice guy and fun to be with and all that, but I'd sure rather be home with my wife and kids than here with him waiting for the snow to melt and the caribou season to open.

I still can't believe we did that!

September 1.

Home! Ray, the pilot, came in late yesterday to drop off three caribou hunters. It took us just about 30 seconds to decide that we wanted a ride out! We were packed and loaded in minutes and we gave up our "Hilton on the Airstrip" to the other hunters. We rolled into Anchorage about four this morning.

Here is what happened. Yesterday, Phil and I slept in again. We had some instant oatmeal for breakfast, and took a walk. Earlier we had seen a few ewes, lambs, and small rams from camp, and a grizzly bear digging a den, but to get to where even they were, we would have to walk about a half mile through deep snow before we could get to a wind-swept ridge. Then we'd have to fight drifts and uncertain footing. Sheep-hunting prospects appeared dismal. The day before, we had seen one small band of caribou. Cows and calves, but this is a bulls-only area.

We walked up the creek and up a side drainage, perhaps 4 miles round trip. We tested the snow, which turned out to be even deeper than expected and very tiring to get through. We found no sheep, no caribou, and no fresh tracks. Nearly all the sign we did find was old and leaving the country.

We had been back in camp long enough to start a fire and go for a pot of water when we heard the plane. We were cold, wet, and tired. The air temperature was hovering around freezing temperature. We were disappointed. We had come to hunt sheep but could not. We were discouraged. We had hoped to get a caribou, but the promise of a successful hunt, after two more days of waiting for the opening day, did not seem good. It was a tough decision. But we were satisfied with it. We were probably in the plane within 15 minutes.

I'm sure it was the best decision.

After all the anticipation, preparation, planning, and expense the greatest disappointment of all was just not even getting a chance to hunt sheep. No hunter expects to always be successful but it is highly unusual for anyone to say that he did not enjoy the hunt. Actually, we ended up with little more than an expensive camping trip. But, as Phil pointed out, maybe it wasn't so bad after all. Lots of people spend a lot more than we did to just lie around and do nothing for a few days. And they fly all the way to Hawaii. We didn't even have to leave Alaska.

P.S. 1. After we returned home, we learned that the storm that hit us was no local weather event. It was the tail end of a dying typhoon that blew in from over the Pacific Ocean and all the way across Alaska, leaving damage and a big dump of snow.

P.S. 2. Talk about a good news–bad news trip. The day after I got home, I came down with a case of Giardia. I probably had gotten infected from some field work I had done near Talkeetna the week before I left on our hunt. I had been helping a crew to pull out a beaver dam that was impeding upstream migration of coho salmon. I can only be thankful that the cramping and diarrhea didn't hit in the middle of that blizzard … or even at our base camp … or on the 10-hour ride home.

Bye for now.

Bill

March 13, 2007

Oh, wait, there is more … Alaska can be a very dangerous and unforgiving place to get around in and Phil and I certainly learned some valuable lessons on this trip.

Alaska is dangerous and unforgiving for several reasons. Much of Alaska is remote. After the plane drops you off and you listen to the sound of the engine fade into the blank sky, you are left in silence with a very lonely feeling. Because you are alone. And on your own. There is no cell phone coverage. We did not even have cell or satellite phones in the 1980s. Until the plane comes back, you are responsible and on your own for whatever happens next.

Weather is always a factor, particularly on multiday trips. Mountains can often create local effects and long-range forecasts are unreliable.

A person needs to plan carefully. Important safety and survival items must be packed. With critical backups: tent, stove, sleeping bag. You can schedule a particular day for a pickup, but the actual time is always weather dependent so plan for two or three extra days of food.

It is important, too, to rely on local networking. Poll your friends to get their opinion and learn from their experiences. I think that pilots and flying today are more reliable than 30 years ago. There is an Alaskan saying: there are old pilots and there are bold pilots, but there are no old, bold pilots.

There are many ways to be killed or injured during outdoor activities in Alaska. When I visited the doctor and learned that I had Giardia, I also learned that I had experienced early signs of hypothermia. A hiker in the Chugach Mountains near Anchorage was caught in this same storm and died from hypothermia.

Flying in small planes is part of hunting in Alaska. This practice is not inherently dangerous, but accidents happen.

A lot of Alaska is more vertical than horizontal and the steeper it gets, the more dangerous it becomes. Sheep and mountain goat hunters and mountain climbers are especially at risk of falling off a mountain. People involved in winter activities, skiers and snowmachiners, when the conditions are right—or wrong—can be especially vulnerable to avalanches.

Cold-water immersion claims victims in Alaska annually. On the ocean and in lakes and rivers. Storms over the ocean may capsize sport and commercial vessels, but rivers are real killers. During winter, frozen rivers are highways for trucks, snowmachines, ATVs, and dog mushers. Unfortunately, river currents and air temperatures convene to continuously form and erode open leads in the ice in a constantly changing cover. Each winter, some snowmachine tracks end at the edge of some open water. During very cold weather, the ice cover may build and tighten causing pressure on the entrapped flow. The water finds a spot of weak ice and escapes to flow over the ice. Not surprisingly, this is called overflow. This is especially dangerous for dog mushers and snowmachiners. Cold and wet is a dangerous combination.

Wild animals have a much worse reputation than they deserve. Nevertheless, they are another hazard for folks in outdoors Alaska. Bears, of course, are the best known-bad guys, but moose, particularly cow moose with young calves, are dangerous. Musk ox and bison can be aggressive. The most important rule ... be aware. Consider the situation and think of ways to avoid an encounter. Make noise. Be visible.

Alaska is big country. Alaska is wild country. There are many ways to get lost. There are many ways that the environment can hurt a person.

The bottom line: plan ahead, ask questions, use a reliable guide, outfitter, or pilot. Ask for references. Use your head and don't take chances.

One last tidbit. During recent years, Alaska has had an aggressive program to improve boating safety and the number of fatalities has been diminishing annually.

Link: Alaska Department of Natural Resources,
Office of Boating Safety
http://dnr.alaska.gov/parks/boating/index.htm

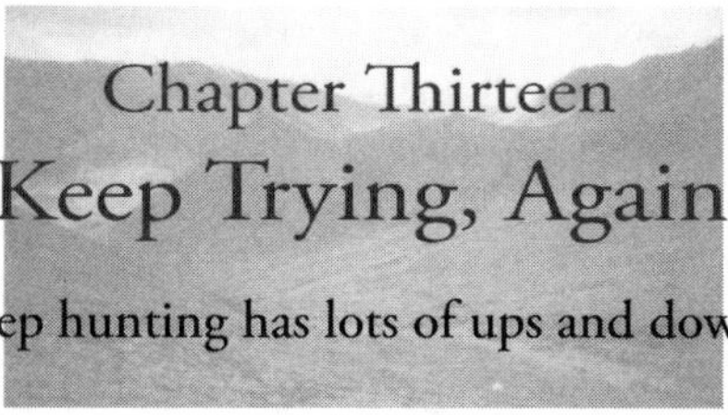

Chapter Thirteen
Keep Trying, Again

Sheep hunting has lots of ups and downs.

Monday, August 26, 1985

Hello.

I have got some time to kill now so I can make a start on my annual letter. We're waiting for the fog to lift from the top of the mountain so we can go look for one of the rams we spotted as we flew in yesterday.

The last week has been real topsy turvy for me. Just one week ago, I learned that Phil, my intended sheep-hunting partner could not make the trip this year–just as I was finishing plans to schedule a trip with the flying service. We had planned go to the same area where we have gone the last two years. I groped around blindly to find a new partner and by Tuesday noon, I had given up and began to plan a duck-hunting trip instead. Then Dave called. He had also planned to hunt here, but one week later. As it happens, his partner had also canceled but he decided he could warp his schedule so he could go sheep hunting with me. Anyhow, Saturday, we drove all night to get to Northway. We flew into this remote Baultoff Creek airstrip by Sunday noon and packed in about 7 miles in 5 hours to set up a spike camp.

Overnight, it rained almost constantly and this morning there is snow on the saddle we had intended to hunt across. Unfortunately, the fog is there, too. It would be dangerous to hunt and it would be easy to get lost. So here we are, waiting in our tent for the fog to lift so we can get out for a walk.

Gosh, I surely would like to get a nice sheep and maybe, later, another caribou.

August 27

Writing time again. Our hunting plan entails hiking upslope from our spike camp about a mile with about 1,500 feet elevation gain. We plan to cross over that saddle, cross the next small drainage, and up to the next ridge. From there, we will work our way down the ridgeline looking for sheep. With this strategy, we hope to approach the animals from above and behind as they typically lie in a good vantage point of their own and look out over the broad valleys below. The bad news is that if we have success we'll have to bring them back up to the saddle from the other side before we can get back to our spike camp.

Essentials for a successful sheep hunt include a good pair of boots, a good tent, and a lightweight pot to boil water.

Well, yesterday afternoon, the fog cleared enough for us to go "take a look." After two hours, we made the top and all went well for about 15 minutes when it started to rain and our visibility went bad. Then it hailed for about 15 minutes; then it started to snow. It took us over an hour to get back down.

This morning, it seemed that the weather was breaking and would turn clear. We got an early start and dashed up the mountain in 1½ hours even though we were trudging through six inches of snow by the time we topped out. But just as we topped out and peeked over into the next drainage, the fog rolled in. We waited for it to lift—about three hours—and waited. We were able to keep warm with our emergency space blankets because there was no wind. Maybe if there had there been some wind the fog would have blown off.

Another lost day. Another disappointment. I guess that is what sheep hunting is all about.

When the fog rolls in, the sheep hunting stops. It is too dangerous to maneuver or even know where you are heading.

Think positive. Tomorrow will be clear.

August 28

This part of this letter is going to be very difficult to write, but I know I must. Today it *was* clear. It is early evening and we're sitting at our spike camp killing time. We got the weather we had hoped and prayed for and got off to an early start this morning. Before we were halfway up the slope and approaching the first saddle, we spotted a sheep. A ram. We didn't get a good first look at it and we wasted nearly an hour before we determined that it was only a sublegal half curl. It did look beautiful, however, on the skyline. And then it just disappeared. We just weren't sure about it. Then, just as we got a better look, it spotted us and it immediately left the country. It is so impressive to see how those animals can move over the talus slopes and up a mountain.

Anyhow, today is the day that I learned that sheep hunting comes with a price tag attached. And, I guess, I just didn't have quite enough change.

We pushed on, according to our strategy, to nearly 6,500 feet elevation and about three miles from our spike camp. We spotted two rams. Below us. Only with a spotting scope could we tell that one was a full-curl legal-sized ram; the other was bigger, about 1¼ curl. They were at least 1,500 feet below us. After we watched them for a while, we realized that our options were few. They had all the advantage.

Our only possible approach was down the next ridge. It would probably take about two hours to get to their level; then we would have to cross a talus slope to get to them—but only if they had not seen or heard us by that time and had not moved off. Talus is very noisy and sometimes dangerous to cross, and sheep have excellent hearing. Our chances of just getting *to* the rams were slim. If we went after them, it was all but certain that we would not make it back to our camp by dark. If we scored, we *certainly* would not make it back.

Dave was ready to go after the sheep. But he was only mildly persuasive. I was cold. The wind was blowing 30 to 35 knots, and we had been in it constantly. Where the sun hit, the snow was melting. In the shade, it was freezing. We discussed our options and evaluated our odds. I was reluctant to take the chance. I recalled my bad experience from the year before. Dave did not push, but accepted my nervousness. We turned back.

It is nice to be in high country, but the going is slow. After I gain elevation, I am jealous of it and hate to give it up until I have to.

About an hour into our retreat, it really hit me what I had just done. Here were the sheep I've been wanting. That I'd hunted for. When I had a chance—a *chance*—I gave up without trying. I teach my kids that they must at least *try*. Perhaps I should listen to my own words. Dave says he is comfortable with our decision. I feel bad that I let him down. If I had been more aggressive, things would have worked out differently. Maybe we would have found success.

Probably tomorrow, we'll head back to the airstrip and assess our chances of getting a caribou or two.

September 2

Right now, we're sitting at the airstrip waiting for Ray, the pilot, to pick us up. Our hunt is over. I think we both feel a sadness that this week is at an end. We've both enjoyed this week even though it has been filled with frustrating ups and downs.

We never did get our sheep. Those we knew of were very remote; we saw no other legal rams. Another party, who also was hunting here, saw no legal rams. Oh my, but the two we found looked regal and elegant through the spotting scope. Without it, of course, they were little more than small white animals with a sort of yellow brown color about their heads.

One day we went up the drainage intending to cross over a different high pass where we could walk around a mountain to look for sheep. We didn't expect to see any, so we weren't disappointed. When we flew in, we saw a few ewes and lambs in the area.

Along the way, we checked out the campsite where Phil and I had been pounded by a storm last year and I salvaged what I could. The tent had a number of rips and tears and I found the one-burner gas stove that had been lost under several feet of snow. I pumped it up and, amazingly, it started on the *first* try! Most of the freeze-dried food was still good, along with some of the other items that were inside plastic bags, including some jerky. Most of the cotton fabric stuff, like clothes, was mildewed, but those which had stayed dry seemed okay. I am especially surprised that a grizzly didn't come along and tear things apart or that the ground squirrels didn't do more damage.

It was more than a little eerie to be there. We had abandoned this place last year after we had been caught in a blizzard. We were lucky to get back to our base camp. Looking at the remains of our camp created some odd feelings and haunting memories. I had to walk around the site twice before I could touch anything.

Yesterday, September 1, was our day to get a caribou. While we were looking for sheep, we had spotted a small band of six to eight caribou and some singles so we knew there were some in the area … as did the other party of hunters. As it turned out, we started earlier in the day than they did so we had the advantage.

Dave worked around to the north along the edge of the stream. I went closer to the foot of the mountain. As we came out onto a large open area of tundra, I spotted three caribou and I could see Dave, too. He was closer and I thought he could get a good shot. I tried to make myself visible to him as I tried to improve my position.

Uh oh! Abruptly, I saw a strange shape in the willows nearby. It was the head and shoulders of a grizzly! At about 75 feet. Standing to get a better look.

At that point, I became somewhat distracted. I lost my concentration on those caribou and completely forgot my strategy. When I waved my arm, the sow grizzly dropped down on all fours, came closer, and stood up again. I whistled. Fortunately, that was enough. She dropped down again and ran off. She was a beautiful blonde with long fluffy hair. Just then, I noticed the movement of a smaller bear beside her

Now, what to do? The bear disappeared over a rise. Should I go and check to see if she had kept going or stopped? No. Should I ignore the bear and go after the caribou? No. First I waited. Then I moved off. Slowly quartering away from the bear and trying to watch out for her and keep my eyes on the caribou at the same time.

At about this time, Dave was just about ready to take a shot at a caribou. For some reason, he became distracted when he saw two bears running across the mountainside! He finally shot. And he had one down. Now the caribou were on alert. They saw bears running—and people. Shooting. And smelled bear. They run. I run to head them off. They run faster.

Well, I never did catch up with them, but someone in the other party did get one. At least, we all got some meat. That bear sure messed up my caribou hunt.

September 6

We made it home all right. The meat and gear are all taken care of. The caribou meat tastes great!

In retrospect, I'm still not certain about our decision not to go after those sheep. For sure, we made the smartest decision. But we got no sheep. Maybe it wasn't the best decision.

As the week progressed the weather improved. I got to know Dave better. As it turns out, he has had a lot of experience with impromptu, or siwash, camps. I became more comfortable again with the remoteness. The psychological impact of the experience from a year ago had lessened. If the opportunity for a sheep had come later in the week, I might have felt differently. Maybe I would have been more willing to take the chance to go for it.

Well, we had a good week. It was a good trip. We had to work hard at times and it had a downer or two, but it was relaxing and it was just a good feeling to be out. Weather conditions were variable and sometimes frustrating, but always bearable.

Anyhow, I got close, again. Be positive. Next year will be the magic year.

Bye for now.

Bill

> October 31, 2008
>
> Oh, wait, there is more ... I recall that during this hunt while we were away from camp, we had an animal break into our campsite and wreak havoc with some of our things. It found a food bag and devoured as much as it could and made off with more.

The food bag was a sack of GORP—Good Old Raisins and Peanuts—and the wild animal that wreaked havoc was an Arctic ground squirrel. Unfortunately, the GORP was inside of some other bags and the ground squirrel chewed its way in. It didn't get too much GORP, but it sure made a mess.

Arctic ground squirrels are the only ground squirrels in Alaska. They are usually about a foot long plus a tail of several inches. They are grizzled brownish-gray in color with some rusty-colored tones. They resemble other ground squirrels with a rounded head, blunt nose, small ears and short legs.

Arctic ground squirrels live in well-drained tundra and meadow areas through a wide range of elevation from sea level to alpine. They eat a variety of plant materials including seeds, roots, bulbs, and leaves as well as insects and bird eggs. They live in colonies in burrows and tunnels and hibernate underground in winter when their body temperature may drop from 98.6° F and supercool to 26.4° F, the lowest known of any living mammal. They mate in the spring and litters are often as many as 10 pups.

It is fortunate that arctic ground squirrels are prolific because lots of animals like to eat them. Grizzly bears are powerfully adapted for digging and they dig avidly for ground squirrels. Wolves, foxes, coyotes, and weasels also relish eating them. Eagles, hawks, and owls pluck them from above. In defense, they have developed separate warning alarm cries for a predator from above or on the ground.

And arctic ground squirrels have not gone unnoticed by humans, either. They are called *tsik-tsik* by Inupiat Eskimos from the call they make when they are alarmed. Historically, Alaska Natives and other native peoples hunted and snared the ground squirrels for food. They not only consume the ground squirrel, but also the food of the squirrel. Arctic ground squirrels harvest roots and bulbs and store them in caches for later use. Some Natives dig up the caches and harvest the harvest. The small bulbs in the squirrel's cache are called mouse nuts. Mouse nuts are eaten boiled or fried in seal oil. Mouse nuts are a valuable addition to the Eskimo diet, rich in carbohydrates, protein, vitamin C, calcium, and minerals.

Alaska Eskimos have another name for arctic ground squirrels. They are often called parka squirrel, because they sew the skins of ground squirrels together to make winter parkas. The parkas are elegant. They are trimmed and decorated with contrasting fur tassels and pieces of leather and include a hood rimmed with a long fur such as wolverine. One report said that it took 45 squirrel skins to make one parka.

Squirrel-skin parkas are highly functional and very warm. Today, however, they are mostly worn for special occasions. I always look forward to attending the sled dog races or the parade during the annual midwinter Anchorage Fur Rondy because many Natives will be there wearing their squirrel-skin parkas. Unfortunately, it is impolite to stare, even if it is in admiration.

One last tidbit. Wolverine fur is often used for the ruff around a parka hood because the durable, soft, flexible hairs repel frost that condenses from breathing.

Link: View pictures of arctic ground squirrels
http://www.nhptv.org/NATUREWORKS/arcticgroundsquirrel.htm

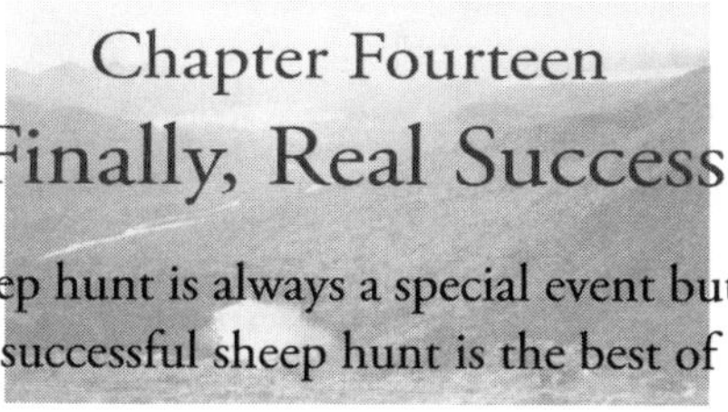

Chapter Fourteen
Finally, Real Success

A sheep hunt is always a special event but the first successful sheep hunt is the best of all.

August 11, 1986

Hello to you.

I hope you are having a fine day. Mine is turning out to be a rather lazy one. Earlier, my friend Phil and I took a short walk up near the glacier to look for sheep. It was mostly an easy walk and the scenery was overwhelming. And there was a special excitement to walk out on the leading edge of the glacier. But, though there were lots of sheep, we saw no legal rams and we could not proceed up the valley as far as we had expected. So we came back to camp, took care of some camp chores, and napped.

You can tell by now that I am on my annual sheep hunt. This time, we are hunting out of Nebesna in the Wrangell Mountains, not far from Wrangell-St. Elias National Park. Yesterday was the first day of the season. I shot my ram at 9:22 a.m. Now we need to find one for Phil.

Let's see … Last Friday, we drove to the village of Nebesna and took an air taxi charter out to Mesa Lake by about 3:30 p.m. We walked until 7:30 p.m. and put in our spike camp. The next day, we started hiking again. We have enough food for eight days and we will be picked up again at the lake on the 17th. Well, on Saturday, we had nearly reached our destination when we caught up with three other hunters who Phil happened to know. They had decided to split up but one guy, Leo, proceeded up the valley ahead of us along the edge of a large, intensely glacially-braided stream. Shortly, we caught up with Leo again. He had his spotting scope lined up on one of three rams across the stream. It was a legal ram! And only a short distance from where we wanted to camp! For some reason, Leo didn't want to pursue this sheep but we kept our eye on it until it was nearly dark. Phil had already told me that I was to have the first shot so this one was mine if I wanted it. It was just a nice, legal-sized, full-curl ram. That was all I was wanting.

I was excited when I got up the next morning. That quickly changed to disappointment when I discovered that the ram was not where we had expected it to be. Soon, however, we located it again and went into action. First, I had to cross the glacial stream. I took off my pants, put on a pair of sneakers, and crossed with my backpack, sleeping bag, and a few other emergency supplies. Phil held back and went downstream to watch the sheep and direct me with arm and hand signals.

I crossed all right, cached my sleeping bag, and headed after the sheep. When Phil gave me a signal to hurry up, I took some rain gear, dropped my backpack, and headed up and around the mountain. Parts of the chase were challenging to say the least. It was steep. Some was rocky and some was talus. Mentally, I asked everyone I could think of for help. I was thirsty and the only water I had was some I caught in a fold of my raincoat as it dripped over a rock.

I could not understand what had happened. I thought I should see the sheep by now. I was tired. And winded. I nearly gave up. Phil had lost his view of the sheep. I decided to try pushing around one more ridge. Wait! There! I saw it. And it was gone! Keep going, carefully, quietly. One more ridge. Where did it go? Phil spotted it again and signaled "Close." Oh no. There it is! It is looking right at me! Freeze! Shrink down, breathe. Get ready! Now. But it's gone! No, there it is! I could find no rock to lean on. I was too low for a sitting shot. Stretch up. Bang! And it was down.

I was very pleased. My first sheep. Not a big ram but a nice one. I had worked hard to get to this moment and I was happy. I was thankful to Phil for giving me this opportunity and his support. I was sad for him because I knew how much he, too, wanted to get his first sheep. I only hope we can find an even bigger one for him this week.

Anyhow, at this point, the good news was that the ram had fallen 50 to 75 feet and stopped. It was lodged in a body-sized depression, probably from where a grizzly had been digging for ground squirrels. Otherwise, it would have fallen and rolled at least a thousand feet down the mountain. The bad news was that it was now up to *me* to get him off the mountain.

I field-dressed it and caped it and went back down and around the mountain about a mile where I had left my pack. Then I started back up. It took me a long time to get it boned out, but I kept at it. Bringing it down was steep. There were three particularly difficult and dangerous spots, especially while carrying a load and crossing rain-slicked grass. In one spot, I had to tie a rope to my pack and lower it before me.

By the time I got back to the stream crossing, it was late afternoon and since the glaciers melt more during the day, the stream was faster, higher, and bigger. I decided I had used up all of my prayers and luck for one day and I would wait till morning to cross.

A spotting scope is invaluable for examining a sheep at some distance to verify its size before you waste time and energy chasing a false lead.

That evening, I dined on broiled fresh sheep meat. Good! I used my space blanket as a ground cloth and a windbreak at my little *siwash* camp in the willows. I slept tired but fitfully and crossed the glacial stream at about six this morning.

On a clear day in high country, it seems that you can see forever.

I guess that brings me up to today. I have so many mixed-up emotions inside it is hard to settle down. I want badly for Phil to get his sheep. I appreciate how he helped me and I will be helping him all week.

Oh, my, I am so stiff and sore and tired. I'm sure glad we didn't push it hard today, but I should be sleeping now, I guess. I am glad, though, that I can share my thoughts and experience with you.

August 15

My goodness, so much has happened in the past four days, I hardly know where to start. As for the present, we are lying in our tent back at Mesa Lake hoping that it will stop snowing so we can get picked up and head back home.

Monday evening, just before dark, Phil spotted Leo at his camp about a quarter mile away and went to see how he had done. Leo had gotten his ram the night before. He had spotted some others and told Phil where to find them. Phil was excited! Boy, was he talking fast!

It seems that Leo had carried his camp to the next higher level of the mountain, saw lots of sheep, searched for a ram, and finally set up a camp. He had just finished supper and inadvertently clanked his spoon in a tin cup. Oops. He looked up carefully. Whoa! He was surprised to discover a legal-sized ram standing about 75 yards away! Watching. He slowly and carefully rolled 25 feet to get his rifle and he shot the ram!

Phil and I started early the next morning. We cached the meat, cape, and horns from my sheep along with extra food and clothes we didn't need. We took the smallest and lightest camp we could and went up the mountain. We walked up a streambed and picked our way through the rocks and cobble. As we neared the top, we made a serious error in judgment and picked the worst possible route, so we had to backtrack and pick another route before we could top out. It took us nearly four hours to climb the 1,500- to 2,000-foot elevation change in just 1½ miles.

When we achieved our goal, we had a huge emotional jolt. On the one hand, the view was absolutely awesome. We were on a high rolling plateau which stretched for several miles in each direction. Massive snow-covered peaks were visible. Snowfields and glaciers were scattered throughout. As we crossed from one side to another, it felt as if we had just come out on the other side of the world. On the other hand, there were virtually no sheep to be seen. It was as if Leo had played a cruel trick on us. It was depressing.

The day was gray and windy and cold. That night it snowed. All we could think of was our horrid experience in that blizzard two years ago. When I lifted the tent flap the next morning, I panicked! The snow was nearly four inches deep! That would make it impossible to find sheep and extremely hazardous getting back down the steep slope! You can imagine my relief when I discovered that it was deep only where the snow accumulated as it had skidded down the side of the tent. There was only about a half inch on the ground. Just a little termination dust.

The day was bright but windy. As the snow melted, sheep began to appear nearly everywhere, popping up like mushrooms. We must have seen 80 sheep scattered through the area. Nearly all were ewes and lambs, but we finally located a band of three rams. Two were legal sized! But they were in the open. There simply was no easy way for Phil to get to them without being seen. So he didn't. What he *did* was put on his overwhites, white coveralls which are actually camouflage on snow. He slowly worked down the side of the mountain toward the sheep. Mostly, he slid on his butt so the seat of his overwhites was just shredded. He approached to within about 200 yards of the sheep before they became nervous. Fortunately, that was close enough. Unfortunately, the biggest ram was farthest away. He got a nice, legal-sized sheep anyway!

We worked hard to cut up the ram, then pack it the mile or so to the camp, break camp, and hurry back down off the mountain. We moved the ram and the camp down to the site of our previous spike camp, where we had cached our other gear. A distance of about 3 miles back down the canyon. Through another snowstorm. We set up our tent again about 9:30 p.m.; the weather turned clear and very cold. It froze hard that night.

The next day we slept in.

About noon we got our loads together and followed the glacial stream back down toward our base camp at Mesa Lake. Our packs weighed more than 100 pounds; I'd guessed mine could have been as much as 120 pounds. It took us 6 ½ hours to cover about 6 ½ miles downhill. We put up another camp about three miles from the lake, but on the low side of a saddle. By coincidence, the best tent site was in the middle of a blueberry patch. They were tasty to snack on, but we sure crushed a lot, too.

This morning we brought a load of meat, cape, and horns to the lake and then went back for the camp. The first load took 2 ½ hours; the second was lighter and we made it in less than two hours. The route again followed a streambed and we had to go over and around so many rocks. My goodness, I am always impressed with what a marvelous invention the human ankle is!

So, again, back to the present. The snow has stopped and most has already melted, but it is cold. It is nearly time for bed, or, I should say, sleep, because I am already in my sleeping bag.

The last week has turned out to be another powerful experience for me. Phil and I have tried so hard for so long to get our first sheep. We are both ecstatic.

We have congratulated each other many times. There have been so many emotional highs. We are both so glad that we accomplished this together.

This is a new area for us. And it is three weeks earlier that we had gone in the past. We've missed the bright colors of the fall tundra, but we've enjoyed the great variety of wildflowers we found. This area is much more vertical and steeper than where we hunted before. And much bigger. There were more hunters here, but this country pretty well absorbed them all. We have seen more sheep—hundreds—and more which were definitely rams—perhaps 25—of these, at least seven were legal sized rams. We have heard of six rams harvested.

It's been a good week. A long hard week. And a short week, too.

Enough. Good night for now.

Personal gear, half a camp, and a sheep make a heavy load. We were lucky that most of our packing was slightly downhill and in the floodplain of a glacial stream.

August 21

Hello again! Last Saturday, the 15th, turned out to be a beautiful day. The snow melted off by noon, so we were excited and anxious to get a ride out and be on our way home. But the home-base lake for the plane was fogged in and the pilot could not take off. So we waited. Another party was picked up by another flying service, late in the day. Our turn came on Sunday.

Saturday night, it froze again, hard, but it was bright and clear. The pilot dropped off another party and picked us up for the return trip. We got out by about noon and hit the road. A beautiful day for a drive.

Are we ready to go again? Phil is. By the second day of the trip, he was saying "Sheep or no sheep, this is my last time." Within an hour of getting off the plane, he had nearly made reservations for next year.

We had a marvelous trip. So many new experiences, new country, and new scenery. There were so many highs and lows, physically and emotionally. We worked hard on this trip and it really paid off. I lost nearly 8 pounds. I surely want to go back again. Maybe not next year, but again. The hunting is exciting. The country magnificent and the meat is excellent.

Thanks for letting me share these experiences with you.
Good bye for now.
Bill

March 14, 2007

Oh, wait, there is more ... Patches of low bushes of fully ripe blueberries were interspersed with the patches of tundra that surrounded our tent sites on this trip. Blueberries, or whatever berries are available, are a welcome addition to the usual diet of freeze-dried meals when you are out on a trip like this, especially with instant oatmeal.

Berries, in fact, are highly important to most Alaskans, especially in rural areas. Berries of all sorts are picked and used as part of subsistence diets. Berry picking is a family affair and a very social activity. We took our young children berry picking, too. One year, my son, Bill, who was then about 6 years old, was proud to show that he had found enough blueberries to cover the bottom of his can. Just as he approached close enough to show his accomplishment, he tripped, fell, and spilled the entire contents.

Blueberries are usually the favorite and our wild tundra blueberries are smaller and much more flavorful than the chubbier and softer commercial version. These wild ones are so much better in pancakes than the commercial berries, and while my family was growing up, I routinely made sourdough pancakes with blueberries every Saturday morning. Even today, when Bill or Donna is home for a visit, I am compelled to make sourdough pancakes for them. I suppose these are a sort of Alaska comfort food.

Alaska Natives make ice cream with berries. But, this is special ice cream, called *agutuk* or Eskimo ice cream. There are various recipes, but one traditional method starts by whipping seal oil with sugar and water or snow until it becomes fluffy; then add berries like blueberries or salmonberries. Chill and enjoy. Crisco may be substituted for the seal oil.

I like lowbush cranberries, too. These are often called lingonberry. They are not true cranberries but they resemble commercial cranberries in color and shape. They usually are only a bit larger than the eraser on a pencil and they can be substituted for cranberries in recipes. By far, I think the best way to use lowbush cranberries is in cookies.

Here is my favorite lowbush cranberry cookie recipe. These are great for the holidays! Commercial cranberries may be substituted for the wild lowbush cranberry.

CRANBERRY COOKIES Makes 4 dozen

- Preheat oven to 375 deg.

- Cream together:

1/2 cup softened margarine

1 cup sugar

3/4 cup brown sugar

1/4 cup milk

2 Tbsp orange juice (use 1/4 cup orange juice for a moist cookie)

- Mix:

3 cups flour

1 tsp baking powder

1/2 tsp salt

1/4 tsp baking soda

- Add to creamed ingredients

- Stir in:

1 cup chopped nuts (optional, but I like them)

1 ½ to 2 ½ cups lowbush cranberries (or chopped commercial cranberries)

1 cup chocolate chips (optional) (I like to add these!)

- Drop onto lightly greased cookie sheets

- Bake at 375 degrees for 10 to 12 minutes

One last tidbit. Blueberries are a great addition to a diet–rich in flavor, nutrients, antioxidants and fiber, but low in calories.

Link: Collecting and Using Alaska Wild Berries,
University of Alaska Cooperative Extension Service
www.uaf.edu/ces/publications/fhepubs.html

Chapter Fifteen
Jim Creek

This easy day hunt took more than a week.

Sunday, September 18, 1994

Hello to all of you.

Today is truly a day for me to say thank you to the guy up above. Yesterday, he truly smiled on me. He gave me a nice moose in the nicest way. And, do you know what? I am not even writing this from some remote camp or an airport. I am at home.

Actually, yesterday began nearly a month ago. My partner, Joe, and I hunted the opening weekend of the moose season near the Buffalo Mine Road, about two hours by road from Anchorage. I had the good luck of winning a lottery drawing permit for a cow moose in this area. We were not far from Palmer. We spent two days in heavy, pouring-down rain. Tree leaves were still green. That makes it hard to see *anything* and we saw little sign. No luck.

Two weeks ago, I talked to John about hunting an area near his home just south of Palmer. John knows the terrain very well, but he does not have much hunting experience. I have a cow permit for the area near his home and he likes to eat moose meat. So away we go.

Joe and I meet John Friday evening. John leads us down a trail that has been heavily used by four wheeler ATV's. After a 15-minute walk, John freezes in mid stride. A cow moose! It is in an open field! I drop my pack. I ease forward. I am able to keep a small tree between me and the moose. She is two steps from the tree line. Carefully. Quietly. Easy. Abruptly, she turns! She steps farther into the field. Now she is broadside to me! No wind. Tall grass. A clear shot! Ready. Now. I line up. Steady. Range 100 to 125 yards. Squeeze.

I should stop right now to avoid the embarrassment. But that would prevent completion of the whole story. We had barely begun to hunt. It all seemed too easy. It was.

I missed.

I missed!

I had tried for a head shot. Dumb. It was a little too far for that kind of shot, the light was too poor, and I did not have a good lean. The haze of light oil that strayed onto the lens of the scope after that day in the pouring rain didn't help either. But I missed. I have made shots that were equally and more challenging, but this time I was embarrassed and frustrated because I missed what should have been an easy shot.

During the next day and a half, Joe saw a small, nonlegal bull and a cow but he did not have a cow permit so he could not shoot. I saw a nonlegal bull, too.

Try again. I contacted Jake, who lived near the Matanuska River bottomlands. I met him one day after work and we checked out an area where he has often found moose. Still no luck.

When I got back home, Bill Jr. asked "Any luck?" "Well," said I, "It was a great evening to be out and I had a chance to look over some very interesting new country." "Oh," he said,"That means you didn't see any." He is becoming wise in his age.

You must understand that this has been a most unusual season for me. I have simply been unable to focus properly. I have felt continuously off balance. Things have been unsettled at work for the last six months or so and there is always something going on with family activities. Anyhow, I have been unable to take vacation time to just concentrate on a serious hunt and the seasons are now earlier than before and it just doesn't *feel* like hunting weather, so, all in all, the focus and intensity have been missing. Once I am out there, I am all right but I forget details.

This brings us back to yesterday. Friday night, I went to the kids' cross country running meet instead of moose hunting. Besides, Joe couldn't go and I'd rather not camp out alone.

I was on the road by 5 a.m. to meet John. We returned to the site where I blew my shot and by 7 a.m., spotted a moose but we could not get a good look. It was far away and the light was poor. We waited and watched and finally went after it but it was gone. By noon, we gave up on it.

We went to John's house for a sandwich and we changed our strategy. We loaded his canoe to try a short float trip. We launched, crossed a lake, and started down Jim Creek. Shortly, we went down a dead-end slough, paddling quietly and watching carefully at every bend even though it was midafternoon and there was little chance of moose moving around. Turn around.

Head back to Jim Creek. About this time I was starting to recall the numerous horror stories I had heard about moose that died in the water. They don't float. And they are big. When they fall, that's where you get them. If they are underwater, that is where they must be butchered.

A hunter would be proud of this moose but can you imagine the challenge of skinning, butchering, and bagging an animal like this if it fell in water, especially in water deeper than this.

Whoa! Suddenly, there is a cow—standing there at a three quarters angle! My rifle is up. I want to shoot but nothing is stable besides the cow. She cannot comprehend what she sees. John does not move. I am trying to get a good sight picture, but it keeps changing in slow motion. I have never seen anything like this before. The canoe is rotating under me. The stern is being pushed to the right by the wind. I am shooting to my front right. The angle keeps getting worse and the difficulty of the shot keeps getting worse. The sight picture keeps changing! Do it! Now! Shoot! She falters. Again! She is running! She is in the water. Splashes and spray everywhere! Boom. She is down. It is over. And she is on *land*! Not in the water! By inches … not feet. We got lucky.

Within five minutes, a canoe with other hunters passed by. Our timing could not have been better.

It took us three hours to butcher and bag the meat. At least, we didn't have to carry it far; about 15 feet. The loaded canoe was heavy and hard to handle in the wind, but it sure was easier and faster than packing it down a trail on our backs, 60 pounds or so at a time.

After we hung John's share at his home and put away the canoe, I stopped and gave Jake a big roast and I gave a front shoulder to Joe. Moose are great because they are big enough for lots of sharing.

I was home by 9 p.m. Just a nice one-day hunt … after several other days of trying.

September 23.

A biologist at the Alaska Department of Fish and Game estimated the age of the cow at two to four years. The estimated live weight was 800 to 900 pounds. That is a lot of protoplasm surrounded by hair, all in one great big lump on the ground. But it was *so* much better on the ground than in the water! Thank you, Lord.

Another hunting buddy, Jim, had a cow permit for another nearby management area. He also got a nice cow the same day I got mine. But he was alone. It took him six hours to butcher and bag the meat. Fortunately, he was able to find someone who could help him get it out to the road.

Till later-Bill

February 19, 2009

Oh, wait, there is more ... moose are one of the icons that help to define Alaska and a mature bull moose is certainly an impressive creature. Only bulls have antlers and the largest palmlike antlers may weigh up to 80 pounds and span a width of up to seven feet. Moose in North America are distributed from western Alaska, across Canada to the east coast and south into New England, the upper Midwest and the central Rocky Mountains, but the largest-sized individuals are routinely found in Alaska.

Healthy adult bull moose weigh from 1,200 to 1,600 pounds and adult cows are 800 to 1,300 pounds. Newborn calves weigh about 30 pounds, but by the start of their first winter, they usually weigh over 300 pounds. Bull moose produce prime antlers after age 6 or 7 and the largest antlers are from moose 10 to 12 years old. In the wild, moose rarely live more than 16 years.

Mating or rutting, is in late September and October. During this time, males eat little while they attempt to accumulate and protect a harem of females until they mate. The breeding males may push and shove each other with their antlers but fatal encounters are rare. Antlers are shed during early and midwinter.

Antlers are bony growths which are regrown each year. A skin with fine hairs, called velvet, covers the structure and delivers nutrients through a blood supply. Just before the rut begins, the blood supply is stopped and the velvet begins to die and loosen. The animal rubs the antlers on vegetation to remove the velvet and the dead bone is the structure of the antler. Antler growth, of course, can be dramatic and considerable metabolism and minerals, such as calcium, are needed annually just to support the growth of antlers.

Moose feed on leaves of birch, willow, and aspen as well as grass and soft leafy vegetable matter including aquatic vegetation during summer. During winter, they eat large amounts of twigs and buds from willow, birch, and aspen. In urban areas, they devastate decorative bushes, mountain ash, and other fruit trees. When food is scarce, they may stand on their hind legs to reach high in a tree and bite the end of a branch, pull it down, and break it to bring the branchlets within reach. On some occasions, moose will scrape the outer bark from young trees for food. The tree becomes scarred and may die. Each day, a mature moose will eat about 40 pounds of browse.

Calves stay with the cows from spring until the fall breeding season and cows are highly protective of their calves. Cows with calves are especially dangerous in the springtime when the calves are smallest. When they are upset, the hackles over the cows' neck and front shoulders will stand up, their ears lie back, and they charge. Fast. They will either run through the target or kick and slash with their heavy legs and large, sharp hooves. People and dogs must be careful when traversing moose habitat.

Adult moose may on occasion be killed by bears, or more frequently, by wolves in packs, especially when snow is deep. Most annual predation, however, is on young moose calves by bears during the birthing season.

Historically, moose have been important to Alaskans as a food source. Native peoples, of course, harvested moose for subsistence food, clothing, implements, and dwellings. Professional hunters supplied moose and other game meat for mining camps, road builders, and roadhouses. Today, moose are harvested by subsistence users and sport hunters. Moose are important to Alaskans in another unusual way because moose on roadways can be a hazard for drivers. Most often, moose are killed or injured, but vehicles are damaged and people may be injured or killed as well.

Moose are important to Alaskans in many ways and numerous research projects are undertaken both in the wild and on captive animals. The Alaska Department of Fish and Game Kenai Moose Research Center is a world leader in moose science. The research center houses 19 moose and 23 caribou inside four one-square-mile pens with 16 miles of tall fencing. Numerous research projects have been completed, many having to do with nutrition and physiology that could not be accomplished with freeranging animals.

One last tidbit. Moose are also found in Europe, in Scandinavia, the Baltic states, and Russia, where they are called elk.

Link: The Alaska Moose Federation–
http://www.growmoremoose.org/home.asp

Chapter Sixteen
A Hard Week on the Tundra

Caribou and caribou hunting are about as predictable as the weather.

September, 2004

Hello.

Wow, this has been an interesting week.

My partner, Hazzy, and I talked in midsummer to plan and schedule our annual caribou hunting trip. We have been hunting together for nearly 15 years, so things have become somewhat routine and we have a good idea of about what to expect. This year, our expectations were severely challenged. There was nothing routine about this trip.

Each year, we routinely apply for special Alaska Department of Fish and Game hunting permits for moose and bison and when, just as routinely, we get none, we call Tim and Nancy at Iliamna Air Taxi to schedule an air taxi drop-off for a caribou hunt. Usually, we have been fortunate to enjoy success on these hunts and we certainly have enjoyed the hunting experience. We were originally scheduled to start this hunt on September 18, but when hunting reports sounded poor, we delayed our departure until Saturday, September 25.

Overnight, on Friday, September 24, we set a new record for earliest snowfall of up to six inches for Anchorage. Another delay.

September 27

It had snowed around the village of Iliamna, too—a one-hour commercial flight from Anchorage—but when we finally landed on Sunday, there was no snow on the runway. We transferred our gear to a de Havilland Beaver floatplane and headed west. There was less snow here than in Anchorage, but, when we touched down on Tim's Lake at about noon, about five miles southeast from the Mulchatna River and about an hour's flying time west of Iliamna, about two inches of snow covered the ground. Whoa. This was a new experience; we had never hunted caribou with snow on the ground, but, we opined, "It should be all right ... they should be easier to see."

We had never hunted from this lake. Only rarely have we hunted the same lake more than once. Our instruction to the pilot was simple, "Take us to a place where the caribou will be tomorrow." Of course, most people can predict the behavior of caribou about as well as they can predict the wind ... which changes many times during a caribou hunt in the Mulchatna basin. Our pilot, George, responded, "There is a big bunch of caribou just west of the Mulchatna River. I think that this north wind will make them want to come this way."

We prepared to set up camp, but we had limited options. Aside from the low alders that rimmed the lake, there were few trees, but nice, level places for a camp were hard to find. George had said, "Why not set up on that great, flat sandy beach? It is well protected from this wind." But, what if the wind changed? We would be here for a week. We proceeded to saw off a dozen or so alders where we found two reasonably flat and level spots. One spot was for our tent and one for our kitchen area. We covered the tent with a waterproof 10-by-14-foot tarp. The kitchen included our table, propane stove, water jugs, food totes, waterproof duffle bags, collapsible cooler, and more. This we covered with a 9-by-10-foot tarp. We pulled the tent tarp low over the tent and the kitchen tarp was raised when we were in camp and collapsed at night and when we were away. This actually turned into quite a comfortable—if cozy—camp, and we only had to carry our gear about 50 feet from the beach, where it was unloaded from the plane. But the snow was vexing.

We had a gorgeous sunset that first evening as we enjoyed our supper of spaghetti with clam sauce. In the evening, the sky was clear. When we awoke the next morning, however, it was solid overcast and snowing, and our enthusiasm was muted by the inch of snow already on the ground. Our start was much slower than usual, but the snow was abating and the temperature was on the rise. In fact, it may have soared to 40 degrees Fahrenheit, so most of the snow melted. But this only made it harder!

Caribou are mostly gray-brown critters with a white rump and a white mane. They live in a mostly gray-brown environment and their bits of white are the best signals we use to spot them. We must have seen thousands of caribou that day. Unfortunately, not one moved and none stood the challenge of a check by binoculars. But the wind was changing and the weather seemed to improve.

We set up a comfortable camp complete with a table, camp chairs, and overhead cover when we fly out to a caribou camp for a week.

A 4-person sleeping tent is more spacious, but a 2-person tent presents a lower profile in wind and rain and it is easier to cover with a big tarp. We trade off a little comfort for a drier tent.

September 28

An instant replay. Another inch of snow on the ground. Finally, about noon, we spotted our first caribou. Three animals. About a mile off. We waited and watched. They simply would not come our way. Later, a herd of 60. Closer; but still, the same results. This terrain was big but very open. There were few trees and the gentle ridges were interspersed with broad valleys. But the snow was nearly gone and the sky had nearly cleared and the wind was abating.

September 29.

Heavy rain. And wind. Probably 40 knots. We could not hunt. The lake level came up about two inches.

September 30

We awoke to find no snow on the ground, but there was a cold north wind. It was getting to be crunch time. Two hunting days remaining and we had not seen one caribou that we could get to. We finished breakfast and began to organize our day packs.

What happened next is straight out of that cartoon that you have seen of a hunter, with eyes as big as plates, straining to reach his rifle as he pulls up his pants while the big buck looks on. Well, we go out and expect to stay for a week, so we try to be comfortable and enjoy good meals, too. Also, we dig a pit and mount a potty ring over it.

That morning, Hazzy just returned from the potty ring and minutes later, I went to take my turn. As I was getting ready to sit down, I heard some wolves howl. They were far away, but it caused me to look around one more time. A caribou! Moving fast, toward the camp! Trotting and pausing and trotting. "Hazzy." "Hazzy!" "Hazzy, bring a rifle!" "Hazzy, caribou!" Finally a reply, but I could not see him through the alders.

Although some mornings it is covered with ice, a potty ring helps make the camp more comfortable and cleaner.

The caribou was trotting. It was nearly past our camp area. I whistled. It stopped! Boom! It was down. In two hours we had it cleaned and bagged and had carried it the 80 yards to our meat cache and we were headed out for more.

It seems that Hazzy heard me when I first called, but he had his first hip boot only half on. He needed to pull it on before he could get ready to shoot. Our timing was perfect. We judged that this all happened within three to five minutes. The caribou would have been visible from the camp vicinity only by someone uphill from the rim of alders around our campsite for a total of about six to ten minutes and only the first few minutes would have allowed a viable response.

This caribou, in the vernacular of our Alaska Natives, truly came to us and gave up its life for us.

October 1

Our last day to hunt. We saw no more caribou until noon. We were getting anxious. We had hoped to have as many as four by this time. A series of low, irregular ridges began about a third of a mile behind the camp and continued for about a mile or so. Our strategy consisted of getting to a vantage point atop the nearest ridge, stand, and look and search with binoculars for an hour or so, or until we became chilled. Then, we would meander over to the next low ridge and go through the same routine. We could probably see five or more square miles from each vantage point. Caribou are not like moose or deer. They are constantly on the move. And it is rare to see one at a time. Where you see them this morning, you will not see them in the afternoon or the next day. Our hope was to peer around the edge of a ridge and find some within range. Or, to spot some in a position where we could move up to them unseen.

There they are! Now, how do we get in front of them? A person certainly cannot catch up by chasing.

We were carefully approaching the top of a ridge farthest from camp. "There! I see six!" But, again, they were in the open. And too far, perhaps 500 yards. All we can do is watch and wait and hope for the best. Thirty minutes. More. They are angling away. Not much hope. What to do? But wait. They turned and disappeared behind a low knob and did not reappear. We decided to take a chance. "What other option do we have?"

We got lucky. We hurried across the open space and dodged around the right side of the hill. There! No. Back. Around to the left. The distance was longish, but doable. One down. Another. When we got to the kill site–oh no, and one more! The last one was a young one which neither of us had shot at intentionally. What is that saying … be careful what you wish for, you might get it.

Now we really had work to do. Hazzy talked me into hauling all this in two trips. We hunt with our backpacks loaded with raingear, an extra layer of clothes, day food, water, emergency gear, and all we need to handle a downed animal. I weighed the packages of meat afterwards and judged that I carried one load of about 90 pounds and one of about 75. More than I have carried for quite some time. Hazzy's loads were similar or, perhaps, heavier. Each one way trip was 1½ to 2 miles (1.14 miles, by GPS). One load took an hour, the other was about 45 minutes. About 80 per cent was gently uphill; ¼ mile was boggy. By the time we were finished, it was 7:30 p.m. And we were exhausted. My feet were numb. Unlike the first one, we had earned these animals.

Usually in camp, we cook special meals and enjoy freshly cooked suppers like barbecued caribou ribs or sweet and sour halibut, but we were beat and neither of us felt much like time to cook anything tonight. We slowly pulled off our hip boots and began to reorganize our gear as we warmed up a hearty, robust soup that Hazzy's wife, Mary, had prepared and frozen for us. Routinely, we plan a good supper for each day, but the schedule is ad lib. Early in the week, we decided to heat the soup for our last evening meal or for an evening when we would get back into camp later than usual. The strategy worked especially well.

We slept well that night.

October 2

It wasn't over yet. Today there was a freezing rain that glazed our tarps. The floatplane arrived at 9:15 a.m. One more glitch. The wind was from the wrong angle. We could not take off safely with a full load, so we had to ferry the meat and one person to a bigger nearby lake. Offload and go back for the other hunter and the rest of the load. Hop to the bigger lake, reload and, finally, we were on our way back to Iliamna.

We saw fewer caribou this year than we were used to, but there were other highlights. Such as the swan serenades—until they had enough of the weather and departed. The numerous flocks of ptarmigan that flashed their white over the tundra. Two red foxes, one of which came left around a low knoll as I moved right … boy, did he run. And, Friday evening, as we ate and packed, a dozen caribou showed up across the lake. They were bright pink in color, illuminated by the bright setting sun.

Another caribou hunt. Hardly a routine trip, but we decided that it was actually a pretty good trip after all.

Talk with you later.

Bill

September 27, 2008

Oh, wait, there is more … Visitors and newcomers to Alaska often ask, "What is tundra?" Or, "How do you describe tundra?"

The Encarta online dictionary defines tundra as the level or nearly level treeless plain between the ice cap and the timber line of North America, Europe, and Asia that has permanently frozen subsoil. Wikipedia says: In physical geography, tundra is an area where the tree growth is hindered by low temperatures and short growing seasons. The term tundra comes from a Russian people Native word that means uplands, and treeless mountain tract. There are two types of tundra: arctic tundra (which also occurs in Antarctica), and alpine tundra.

This is important. There are two kinds of tundra. One is a result of altitude; another is because of latitude. Alpine tundra is all around us. There is some just on the upper edge of Anchorage. It is also found in the high altitudes of most mountain ranges. Arctic tundra is far more widespread in Alaska and caribou are animals of the arctic tundra.

What do we actually see when we look out over the tundra? Usually, when we land on a small lake in a floatplane, the first thing we encounter is a lake margin rimmed with a miniature but dense forest of alders. Sometimes patches of tall grasses intermingle with the alders. After we find a pathway to higher ground, we look for a flat space where we can set up our sleeping tent. Next, we try to locate our kitchen area where we can look out on the lake or the open spaces beyond our camp area. This is the open tundra.

We don't know if permafrost is underground here, of course. You can't tell by just looking. We see wide open spaces, not unlike the Great Plains in the Lower 48. Except that the vegetation is different. Close in by camp and in some wetter areas, gullies, and folds in the land, trees are not unusual. The tallest trees are, perhaps, 10 feet tall. Mostly alders but some stunted, scattered willows, too. Sometimes a few need to be sacrificed to open some space for our camp.

The lay of the land at first appears to be flat, but it soon becomes rolling and it seems to go on forever. As we wander farther from the lake margin, the only trees are willows, some of which are not more than six inches or so in height. Some ground is covered by low bushes that turn out to be a dwarf birch that may be about two feet high. These are interspersed with patches of blueberry bushes. Some areas have more than others. We encounter white patches of lichens which are prime food for caribou. Low, wet areas are white with tundra cotton. Patches of lowbush cranberries, crowberries, and dwarf dogwood pop up here and there. These usually grow close to the ground.

Permafrost may control the subsurface, but the surface area is busy and active. The tundra can be easy to walk over, but, in places it may be boggy and sometimes it has wide spaces of tussocks. There are no tall trees and there are no wait-a-minute vines. It is just big country. You need to be very aware of where you are and how to get back to your camp. A GPS is valuable here. The deceptively flat country is rapidly transformed into a rolling, hilly terrain which, before you know it, can sucker you into another portion of hilly terrain that can isolate you from your camp and send you into lost status.

When we arrive for a caribou hunt, the colors are usually in the midst of change. There are few greens. There are lots of browns. If we are lucky, the colors are changed. The willows are yellow and the birches and dogwood are red.

If we are lucky, the wind will not be excessive and tear up our camp. If we are lucky, the wind will be breezy enough to keep the mosquitoes and blackflies at bay. If we are lucky, the floatplane flights will be on schedule.

This is the tundra. This is where we camp. This is where we hunt. This is where we relax and enjoy just being outside in Alaska. It is wonderful.

One last tidbit. Arctic tundra may seem to go on forever in a horizontal plain. Alpine tundra may extend only a short vertical distance.

Link: Iliamna Lake is the largest lake in Alaska. It reportedly has a monster much like the Loch Ness monster - http://www.alaskascienceoutreach.com/index.php/features/sis_parttwo/what_lies_beneath_lake_iliamna/

Section Four—Travel Alaska

Chapter Seventeen
A Trip to Alaska

We enjoy sharing Alaska with visitors
because we, too, get to visit this great state.

May 27, 2008

Good morning.

How are you doing these days? Karel and I are doing just fine and starting to relax a bit. We have been busy for the past several weeks making final preparations for our trip to Alaska. Now, we are beginning to reap the benefits.

Just now, I am waiting for her to wake up. The alarm will ring in 35 minutes. I woke up early and my brain started to replay some of the events of yesterday and I just had to start this note to you.

I am in our modest hotel room in the McKinley Park Village. There are probably several thousand people right now in this village just outside Denali National Park and Preserve. Less than a month ago, there were, perhaps, fewer than 50 people; less than a month from now, the population may double; but, by the end of September, the number will again be approaching 50.

This village exists as a commercial center to support activities in and around Denali Park. I suppose a gas station and a café may be open during the winter to accommodate winter travelers who are driving between Anchorage and Fairbanks, but, otherwise, this is little more than a fancy summer work camp. It includes nice hotels and simple motels and cabins. Restaurants and cafes. You can arrange for flightseeing, river rafting, bus rides, gold panning, and more. Seasonal help is imported from all over. It is always fun to ask a server, a clerk, or a bus driver, "Where are you from?" "Denver," or "Southern California," or, "New Mexico," or, "Cleveland" may be the answer. Rarely, "Alaska." Many are college students who need a summer job.

I am gazing, now, through our front window. I did not expect to see Mt.

McKinley from here, but I thought we would have a better view than we actually do. Today, this meager view is obscured even more by a low-hanging fog. Twenty-four hours ago, the sky was bright and deep blue and the temperature was about 29 degrees Fahrenheit. I was optimistic that we would see the mountain yesterday during our bus ride into the park.

Although we never did see the mountain because a dense cloud hovered around Denali all day, we did enjoy the National Park tour along the 53 miles of the dusty park road that is currently passable for the tour bus operators. We saw a great variety and abundance of wildlife, such that Karel and I have never had before.

The collective "we" includes a total of six people in our party. Karel and I are hosting the 40-year reunion of her graduating class of dietetic interns from Henry Ford Hospital in Detroit. There were six in the class; three are here besides Karel. Melba is from Australia (originally from California), Sari (Rosario) is from New York City (originally from the Philippines), and Jane is currently from Wisconsin (and has lived in three or four cities in the last 40 years). Jane's husband, Don, is with us, too. What a fun and lively group!

Wow. Yesterday we saw wildlife galore! We had good looks at the Big Four: Dall sheep, caribou, moose, and grizzly bear. We saw willow ptarmigan, snowshoe hares, hoary marmots, picas, and more. They were just beside the road. One small band of caribou crossed the road a hundred yards in front of our bus. The closest bear sighting was several hundreds of yards away.

Oh, good, I just noticed that the fog is thinning and lifting, but a light breeze is pushing it around and everything is drippy wet. Hopefully, the weather will improve.

But the sheep. Dall sheep usually appear as small white dots high on the

We had close up views of Dall sheep, including ewes with lambs in late May. We also saw moose, caribou, and grizzly bears along with a variety of small mammals and many birds.

mountain slopes. Among other sightings, we found a group of eight mature rams only about a hundred yards from the road. One had thin, short, ewe-like horns and one was a full-curl. Most were half-curl or more in size. They were lying down, calmly chewing their cud and surveying the broad canyon below. It was a great treat to see these so close.

But wait! Just down the road, we spotted several ewes. As we watched, another appeared. And another. Look! One has a small lamb. We strained for a better view. There! Another lamb! Ewes were busy feeding, and the lambs stole the show as they hopped down the slope on their springy little legs, dashed around the bushes, and chased each other back up the hill. Two head-butted each other. This was all going on within distance of about 150 feet.

We had arrived at the Park the day before by the Alaska Railroad from Anchorage in a dome car so we were able to enjoy the grand vistas and narrow river valleys along the route. We did see several moose and black bears. Twice, a sow with cubs. It is a great way to travel.

Talk with you later.

The 53-mile gravel road into the Denali National Park offers many places to pull out for a good view. Most visitors travel on tour or school busses.

May 28

As it happens, we returned to Anchorage on the Alaska Railroad. We had arranged to return by a private bus operator, but by a quirk, we ended up traveling back on the train. We like to travel by both road and rail because, although they parallel each other, the views and the experience are quite different. The railroad is a great way to travel, especially in the dome cars with a panoramic view.

We certainly hit it big on our Denali trip. We did miss out on seeing a wolf. A wolf sighting, however, is a rare experience. On average, a wolf is seen at a

The Alaska Railroad is a fun, comfortable, relaxing way to travel between Anchorage and Denali Park and to enjoy the scenic views.

rate of about three per month. There are several reasons why we saw so many animals. The weather had been very good. Mostly sunny, with little wind. The leaves are just beginning to develop so we had good viewing conditions. Also, it is breeding season for many of the birds and animals, so they, themselves were more active and visible. I would like to return in late August when the tundra is in full fall colors and the antlers of the moose and caribou are fully developed.

June is the least rainy month in Interior Alaska and the best month to get a view of Mount McKinley, the tallest peak in North America at 20,320 feet tall.

The mountain is seen by about a third of the visitors annually. The best time to see Denali (the "Great One," in the Athabascan language) is during June, our least rainy month. This part of our trip was punctuated by a remarkable view of the mountain as we floated south on the train. Early in our return trip, clouds filled the space to the west, where the mountain was supposed to be, but later, we were rewarded with several views when the mountain came out in full glory! The air was clean and clear and Denali, along with Mount Foraker and Mount Hunter poked tall and imposing as they anchored and dominated the Alaska Range. What a wonderful way to end our wonderful trip to the park.

May 30

Yesterday, at 10:20 a.m., we boarded the tour vessel *Chugach* for our day-long tour through Kenai Fjords National Park. And what a grand tour we had. The seas had been rough for most of the previous week, but yesterday the weather changed and the wind began to blow from the north. Previously from the south, the wind had been building as it crossed the North Pacific Ocean; yesterday, it was blowing off the land and the water surface lapped with a gentle one- to two- foot chop and only gentle swells.

We spent the night before at a wilderness lodge on Fox Island, a dozen or so miles into Resurrection Bay from Seward. It was like a gigantic bed and breakfast, but it also included a gourmet supper as a bookend to the gourmet breakfast prepared and served by a chef and staff for the total of ten overnight guests. The view and the service were incredible. We were lulled to sleep by the gentle whoosh of the surf and awoke to the marvelous view of the bay that included dots of islands and spruce-filled mountain slopes that were capped with snow and bisected by glaciers. Our only disappointment was that we missed out on an evening paddle in sea kayaks.

The view from the lodge on Fox Island was a grand, broad seascape and the seas in Resurrection Bay settled dramatically as the day progressed.

As soon as the *Chugach* crossed to the west side of Resurrection Bay from Fox Island we began our marine wildlife, coastal Alaska safari. It began with bald eagles and killer whales, or orcas. We saw, perhaps a dozen orcas during the day. Good, but not great views. And humpback whales; one surfaced to breathe within about 150 feet from the starboard bow. Harbor seals, Steller sea lions, Dall porpoises riding the bow wave, black bears, mountain goats with newborn kids. Birds: black-legged kittiwakes, mew gulls, and glaucus-winged gulls, common murres, pelagic and red-faced cormorants. Both tufted and horned puffins by the hundreds! Puffins swimming close to the boat. Puffins diving. Puffins flying high and low. Perched on the rocky cliffs. They were everywhere.

Seabirds, harbor seals, sea otters, Orcas, sea lions, humpback whales, and Dall porpoises are frequently seen during tours of Resurrection Bay.

And glaciers, of course. Glaciers clung tightly to the mountainsides in all directions. Most were mountain glaciers perched high on the slopes and snaking down from the Harding Icefield. Some were valley glaciers, independent of the icefield. But the most spectacular were the tidewater glaciers. The

In some areas, tufted and eared puffins seemed to be everywhere, swimming by the boat or flying between their nesting burrows and feeding areas. Cormorants and other seabirds were nearby.

Chugach pushed through a cluttered mass of floating chunks of glacier ice to the end of the Northwestern Fjord until we were two miles—it seemed much closer because the air was so clear—from the face of Northwestern Glacier. We all crammed against the rail for photos and strained to see an icefall or a calf plunge from the face of the glacier and spray a huge plume of water. Instead, we only heard the glacier groan and grumble as it forced its way to the sea and we heard the great splashes as ice fell from its snout.

Harbor seals with pups decorated the icebergs in front of the glacier and sea otters lolled where there was enough open water. We did see some icefalls, but none of the big calvings that Karel and I have seen during other trips. As we returned, we spotted more black bears and mountain goats with kids. Eagles and eagle nests. It was a long day on the water, but it was another good day.

June 4

We are home now, but that was not yet the end of our trip to Alaska. We stayed two nights at the Tern Lake Inn Bed and Breakfast, an elegant but relaxing home in a magical Alaska setting. We went to Seward on May 30 and we toured the Alaska SeaLife Center, where we found ourselves eyeball to eyeball with Woody, the 2,000-pound Steller sea lion, and a wingspan away from tufted and horned puffins and other seabirds. On the lower level, we watched as the puffins and common murres flew underwater to find their food.

At the Alaska SeaLife Center in Seward you can be up close and personal with Woody, the 2,000-pound sea lion and you can watch puffins and common murres fly underwater as they search for their food.

That evening we made a special supper at the Tern Lake Inn that was dominated by king crab legs and recently caught halibut. The next morning, after a breakfast of crème brûlé French toast and fruit, Karel drove back to Anchorage with Sari while the rest of us met Andy for a Chinook salmon-fishing trip on the Kasilof River (Bending Branches Guide Service). We did not enjoy the fishing success that we had hoped for, but we did have two good hits that we were unable to capitalize on. Nevertheless, we enjoyed the slow, relaxing drift downstream while we chatted away and watched the other anglers and the eagles soaring by—one within 20 feet of the bow of the boat. We drove on to Homer, out onto the Homer Spit and, quite literally to the end of the road, where we had a panoramic view of Kachemak Bay from our hotel room at Land's End Hotel. Another good day.

Karel rejoined us in the morning and we drove around Homer until midafternoon, when we decided should go out for supper. Except, in this case, going out for supper took on a whole new meaning. We elected to have supper at the Saltry Restaurant in Halibut Cove. Nearly 8 miles across Kachemak Bay. By water taxi. Again, there were seabirds and sea otters and glaciers and more in-your-face scenery. The tasty and filling supper was a wonderful way to end our last full day on the road together.

We covered a lot of ground during our nine-day tour of Alaska and we were rarely without a view of mountains or water, fresh and salt, snow-covered slopes or some wildlife. After a trip like this, one is tempted to say that we saw Alaska; however, I like to remind visitors to be careful. From Denali to Seward and Seward to Homer, the road distance is about 540 miles. This means that if you make this trip and report that you have seen Alaska, it is similar to driving from Chicago to Memphis and saying that you have seen the eastern third of the Lower 48 states.

The day-ferry ride across Kachemak Bay shows off scenic views including the seabird rookery on Gull Island and this natural arch at the entrance to Halibut Cove.

All in all, we had a wonderful time with our company and we always look forward to hosting more visitors. Karel and I are already planning our next trip to Alaska.

Keep in touch.

Love from Alaska.

Bill and Karel

October, 2008

Oh, wait, there is more … About every year or so, we get an inquiry from a relative, an acquaintance or just someone we meet that goes something like, "When is the best time to visit Alaska?"

Wow, that is an easy question. But, as usual, there is no simple answer. I usually reply with something no one likes to hear, "It depends on what you want to do." But then I point out that the state is so large and there are so many choices that you need to prioritize. If you look at a map of the United States, you will usually find Alaska appearing as a small island, not far from Hawaii, floating in the Pacific Ocean just off southern California. In reality, the land mass is just about equal to one-third of the Lower 48 states. If you come to Anchorage, for example, and drive to Fairbanks, you may say that you have seen

Alaska. But that is about equal to driving from San Francisco to Los Angeles and saying that you have seen the western third of the United States. Anyhow, here goes.

Getting started. Find general visitor information at http://www.alaskaone.com/ and other web-based sources. Check out the Alaska Magazine (www.alaskamagazine.com) and, for loads of information about Alaska, visit http://www.alaska-visit.com/.

I have limited information about southeastern Alaska, but a visitor should consider a stop at the capital city, Juneau, with the Mendenhall Glacier and Sitka, with Totem Park and the site where the ownership of Alaska was passed from Russia to the United States. Glacier Bay is pristine wilderness. Cruises on the Inland Passage are a wonderful way to see southeast Alaska. Or take a poor man's cruise on the State Ferry system (http://www.dot.state.ak.us/amhs/).

Closer to my home in southcentral Alaska, you can also find many options; so, what do you want to do and see? (http://www.alaskavisitorscenter.com/)

Mountains, glaciers, and lakes. Head south along Turnagain Arm toward the Kenai Peninsula (www.kenaipeninsula.org). You may see white Beluga whales in the glacially turbid waters and watch for white Dall sheep in the mountains. Count the glaciers and moose that you see along the way.

Oceans, glaciers, marine mammals, and mountains. Tour Resurrection Bay and Kenai Fjords National Park from Seward (http://www.nps.gov/kefj/index.htm). The most scenic part of the trip is after about an hour's cruise, so I recommend that the all-day tours are more rewarding than the half-day trips. Check out the Alaska Sea Life Center (www.alaskasealife.org). Or drive to Homer and just admire the scenery as it unfolds along the way, but be ready for the pullout for the big panoramic view just as you round the last big curve. Drive, literally, to the end of the road on Homer Spit. Here you can arrange for any number of small trips across Kachemak Bay to the villages of Seldovia or Halibut Cove or take a sea kayak tour.

Outdoors. Hiking trails and campgrounds abound in Chugach State Park and the Chugach National Forest (http://

www.fs.fed.us/r10/chugach/). State Parks and the National Forest have public-use cabins for rent that are accessible by hiking, floatplane, or canoe. Several glaciers wait patiently if you want to walk on one. Another choice is to take a flight across Cook Inlet to watch brown, or grizzly, bears fishing for salmon. Of course, you can go fishing yourself for the five species of salmon, rainbow trout, Dolly Varden, arctic grayling, and halibut. You just have to decide what you want and when is the best time (www.sportfishingkenai.com). You can arrange for a guided trip or you can head out on your own. Whitewater rafting is available, too, or pan for gold at the former mining towns of Crow Creek or Hope.

Lodging is available from B&Bs, hotels, lodges and restaurants and specialty coffee vendors abound.

Travel north to Denali National Park by auto, bus, or the Alaska Railroad (http://www.nps.gov/dena/index.htm). You might not see the tallest mountain in North America, but you can try for the wildlife grand slam: moose, caribou, sheep, and grizzly bear; and, if you are lucky, a wolf. Go on to the Fairbanks gold country (http://www.explorefairbanks.com/) and Chena Hot Springs (http://www.fairbankschamber.org/).

Palmer and Wasilla are an hour north of Anchorage (http://www.palmerchamber.org/). This is the historic destination of early colonist farmers who were recruited from Wisconsin and Minnesota in 1935. Tour the Reindeer Farm, museums, the Iditarod headquarters, and Hatcher Pass Independence Mine State Park. This is an easy drive to alpine areas. You can also travel east on the Glenn Highway for an hour or two to Sheep Mountain. Have lunch at Sheep Mountain Lodge or Long Rifle Lodge, where you have a panoramic view of Matanuska Glacier. You can walk on the glacier or drive to Eureka Summit. This is a magnificent drive when the tundra and birch trees are flush in glorious fall colors.

Talkeetna (http://www.talkeetna-chamber.com/directory.php?cid=16), north of Wasilla about an hour, is an eclectic historic mining town with interesting tourist accommodations and spectacular views of Mount McKinley on a clear day. This is the jumping-off site for the climbers trying to summit the mountain and you have the option of a flightseeing tour.

And, of course, Anchorage (www.anchorage.net). Unique Alaska souvenirs. Great museum. Walking trails. Hotels and restaurants. Chinook and coho salmon fishing is available when in season, with just a short walk from downtown. You can find help to plan the rest of your itinerary on state and federal lands site (http://www.nps.gov/aplic/). Anchorage is a great place to visit although some locals argue that the best thing about Anchorage is the opportunity to fly out to the real Alaska.

It is a short flight to Kodiak. It is a little known secret that Kodiak is actually the northernmost Hawaiian island (joke). Take a longer flight to Nome or go farther north to Kotzebue or Barrow and cross the Arctic Circle. Or simply take a short flight for fishing or flightseeing.

If you visit during the summer you will have seemingly endless sun, but winter is fun, too. Enjoy world-class cross-country and downhill skiing, snowboarding, and snowshoeing. Snowmachines and dogsledding. The Fur Rendezvous, or Fur Rondy, our winter carnival, begins in late February and includes a carnival, fireworks, parade, the fur auction, and many other events including the World Championship sprint sled dog races. This is followed by the start of the 1,000-mile Iditarod sled dog race. View the aurora borealis as it winds its way through a clear star-filled sky. Winter is a wonderful time to be in Alaska.

What to do while in Alaska, the Great Land? There is much more that I have not been able to include. There are just too many choices.

One last tidbit. No matter what, do bring lots of film and maybe a small pair of binoculars

Link: The Alaska Public Lands Information Centers includes statewide information for planning outdoor activities.
http://www.nps.gov/aplic/

Chapter Eighteen
The Alaska Highway

In the summer of 2000, my daughter, Donna, bought her first car. Then it was time for her to return to the University of Washington in Seattle. One good way to get a car from Anchorage to the Lower 48 is to drive it down the Alaska Highway.

August 20, 2000, 9:30 a.m., Glenn Highway, Milepost 57

Hello.

Donna and I are just now on our way. Only about 2,500 more miles to go. We are on our way to Seattle in her little Honda Civic (1997, red), which she bought five weeks ago.

On our right is the braided glacial floodplain of the Matanuska River. The water surface glistens silver in the sunlight, but below the surface we know it is

Portions of the Alaska Highway are boring, but other parts offer magnificent views.

colored deep gray from a heavy load of glacial silt. Farther to our right, the north edge of the Chugach Mountains rises abruptly from the valley to spire points. The highest points have a fresh dusting of brilliant white snow—termination dust—which signals the end of the Alaska summer. The Talkeetna Mountains on our left and to the front also display several tall points, each with their own show of termination dust.

It is partly cloudy, becoming clearer. A windless, beautiful day! We are on our way down the Alaska Highway to Seattle.

August 20, 5 p.m.

We are in Canada. The weather is improved. The road is not. Numerous potholes and stretches of loose gravel and rough road have slowed our average speed. We passed an incoming big highway truck just as it emerged from a gravel stretch and Donna's bright little red Honda just got its first two windshield dings. In the vicinity of the border, there were extensive wetlands and we saw several swans and cygnets. Here, the spruce trees are taller and the mountains are closer. Donna is driving, dodging potholes and singing along with an Arlo Guthrie CD. We hope to make 500 miles today.

End of day. Alaska Highway, Milepost 1,147; elapsed miles: 525

August 21, Donna writes:

Dad says he'll drive for a while if I write in the letter so …

We're still on the Alaska Highway making our way to Watson Lake. We entered a small part of British Columbia but swiftly reentered the Yukon Territory. Right now, we are bordering the Rancheria River, which reminds me of Alaska's Kenai River and it makes me miss home. The kind of beauty I love about Alaska can't be beaten by many other places I've seen. This is a fun new adventure but I'm sure I will be tired of this highway by the time we reach Seattle. I suppose 10 or 11 hours of driving for four or five days will do that! I am very impressed by the quality of the Alaska Highway south and east from Haines Junction.

August 21, 4:19 p.m., Alaska Highway, Milepost 562 (km 400)

I'm tired. I'm glad that I finished my second shift of driving at Watson Lake. We have traveled easterly for two days. Now we are headed south. Mostly, the road has been quite good. In fact it is getting better … except for the road construction we have just now. Now, 10 miles of good gravel … now, worse. We had been making good time, but this will hurt our average speed. Today has been a good and a troubling day. It has been a good day because we were doing so well. Traveling fast on a good highway. Making good time and feeling good (until the construction which slowed us). But, we also had some troubling information. (Wow! The highway is great here.) First, we discovered from our guidebooks that a quarter—over 100 miles—of the Cassiar Highway is not paved and that the highway is used by logging trucks. On the other hand, the route of the Alaska Highway is 135 miles longer than the Cassiar Highway route to the border. We had planned to take the shorter route until we contemplated the unpaved road and the logging trucks. Other travelers have reported that the route is beautiful. Finally, after we decided to stick with the Alaska Highway, we discovered that the actual distance is several hundred miles longer than our original, pretrip planning estimate! Bummer.

A trip on the long Alaska Highway is an adventure in itself. It required 44 hours of steady driving during four days to travel the 2,300 miles from Anchorage to Seattle.

We just now have crossed a major divide. We had been following the Tetlin River, which drains north and then west to the Yukon River and 2,200 miles downstream to the Bering Sea and the North Pacific Ocean. Now we are in the Mackenzie River drainage beside the Laird River canyon, which drains 2,650 miles north to the Beaufort Sea and the Arctic Ocean.

August 22, 8 a.m., Alaska Highway, Milepost 380

Well! We certainly had an amazing start for today! Yesterday ended somewhat drearily in a cold, blowing rain. We elected to not set up the tent but took a "rustic" kitchenette so we could get a good shower and use a phone. A matter of only 20 or 30 minutes before we stopped for the evening, we were pleased to see a black bear. Another. Then, another. Three in a distance of about one-half mile. Donna happened to be driving, so I was lucky to have better viewing. The first bear was tan—almost grey. The next was a pretty, small, dark black animal and the third one was larger. (We have emerged from the mountains now and in an hour we will be in Fort Nelson.) We were pleased to have such a treat, but within another 30 minutes, Donna spotted a lynx as it stepped across the road from left to right. It stopped, patiently waited, and showed itself briefly beside the road before it turned and folded into the bushes. Wow, that was a *great* treat!

It is always a treat to see wildlife, but I've been told by many travelers on the Alaska Highway that they rarely see any. And today, only 10 minutes after we started, we spotted a deer–a pretty red-coated doe. Ten minutes later, two caribou. Ten more minutes, two more caribou. And some sheep. Stone sheep, two ewes, three lambs, and a small ram! More caribou. Wow! We had seen some small dots of white Dall sheep on a mountain beside Kluane Lake, too. Much more wildlife than I had ever expected. More numbers and more variety. (Eventually, later in the trip, we saw more caribou, a coyote, and moose, too!)

We are just now at about the midpoint of our trip. At Toad River, British Columbia, we had traveled 1,145 miles and we forecasted 1,218 remaining. We have been traveling generally southeast. From Fort Nelson, however, we will head more south; then southwest toward Vancouver and Seattle.

August 23, 10 a.m., Route 97, Milepost 134

We have entered the Fraser River Valley. Headed south. Actually, southwest. Through Prince George. On to Cache Creek. And the border at Abbottsford; then 116 miles to Seattle. The land is so very different! Tall pines, sagebrush, tall spruce. Big rivers, ranches. So many more people, businesses, and towns. The area has a long history of fur trapping, gold mining, and lumbering. Last night was substantially warmer than our first night, which we spent in the rain in our tent at Kluane Lake. Fifteen hundred miles brings many changes.

The signpost forest at Watson Lake, Yukon Territory is estimated to contain more than 54,000 signposts that people have brought from around the world.

Donna's little Honda is doing well. I suppose it should. Donna—whoa—quick stop for a potty break at Williams Lake. Donna treats her little car nicely. And she talks to it nicely, too, as she pats it gently on the dashboard.

Here, the Milepost Travel Guide (which documents the mile location and describes some interesting or important info) is of little value. It does not have the detail that it did farther north. Here, for example, gas stations appear spontaneously every 10 miles or so. In the north, they may be 80 to 100 miles apart, so the Milepost is very useful for planning ahead. Roads here are predictably better. Bottom line, however: Don't leave home without the book. For this trip, we really put it to good use. It is indispensable to schedule and plan when and where to find gas, an outhouse, groceries, places to sleep, and camping sites. It warns of bad reaches of road conditions and steep grades. It is updated annually and loaded with local information, history, natural history, industry, and lore.

Now, about 250 miles north of the border with the United States, there is lots of rangeland. Cattle, horses, hay making. Lumber trucks have largely disappeared from the highway. Oops, another pause for a construction zone.

August 26. Continental Flight 125

Where should I begin, except to say, that this is the end—or nearly so—of the trip. Donna should be "home" by now. She brought me to the Sea-Tac Airport where we said our goodbyes and she returned with her red 1997 Honda Civic to her apartment. Alone.

We did have a great week together even though it was a busy, intense week. Four long days of driving and three busy days of collecting and moving her belongings to her apartment and starting to get ready for school.

I cannot say that driving the Alaska Highway was fun, but it certainly was a unique experience. Most of the scenery was beautiful. Some was boring. It was all special. We were a team. And this trip requires teamwork. It would not be a nice or fun trip to do alone. It was 2,312 miles in 44 hours of driving over a four-day period. Ten to 12 hours of driving each day. We were focused on the driving. We stopped for gas, sleep, and potty. At least one more day would have been better to have enjoyed the trip a bit more. But we were unsure of the time and timing. We drove. We enjoyed the scenery and the changes of the landscapes, the rivers, the mountains, the towns, the people, the vegetation, and the highway through the windshield. The driver concentrated on the car and the road. The passenger provided extra observation, updates from the Milepost, food and beverages. A long, intense trip that went fast.

I was not anxious to start the trip, but I am glad that I went and glad that I was able to be with Donna and that I was able to help her. She will now have a few days to settle into Seattle and her apartment before her classes begin at the University of Washington. I will return to work. It already seems long ago that we set off on our trip, which seemed endless at times, but which in retrospect went by so quickly.

Karel reported by phone that since we have left, the termination dust has been more frequent, getting lower on the mountains, and looking more serious. And that the moose have cleaned out the garden.

As Donna said, she looked at a map with a long squiggle line that traced our origin in Anchorage to our destination in Seattle, "Wow, we have come a long way … "

Love from Alaska and other points,

Bill and Donna and Karel and Bill, too!

August 31. Anchorage, Alaska

P.S. Back at home. The termination dust has retreated. There is no new snow lingering in the Chugach Mountains. The moose sure did eat up the broccoli and stomped all over the carrots in the garden.

Talk with you later.

Bill

> March 2, 2004
>
> Oh, wait, there is more … the claim of having traveled the Alaska Highway is an extra mark of distinction on one's resume as an Alaskan. Most often, a trip "on the Highway" is not for the recreation, but it is still an adventure. Over the years, as the population of Alaska has swelled and air travel has improved, it seems that a smaller percentage of the population can make the claim. I nearly missed out, myself, but I did enjoy the trip and I look forward to making it again with my wife, Karel.
>
> I have listened to numerous tales about driving the Highway. Most are favorable, but it is interesting how things have changed over time. The Highway, when we drove it in 2000, was, I think, actually paved for its entire distance. The unpaved stretches that we encountered seemed to be rebuilding and repaving sections that had been previously paved. Any road needs constant maintenance and reconstruction and this one is no exception. Obviously, the bad sections of pavement were some of the earliest paved sections and will probably be repaved in the next several years.
>
> The reconstruction efforts have led to some interesting changes. During the process, hills are reduced and big bends in the route are cut off and, as if by magic, the length has been shortened! Not by much, of course, but enough to create some curiosity. In some stretches, the mile markers identified in the

Milepost disagree with those posted along the road. Many historic roadhouses and other buildings proudly display the mile number as they have for many years but these, too, disagree with the mile markers on the highway or in the book. To make matters somewhat more confusing, the mileage in Canada is presented in the metric system! The good news is that the confusion is actually more humorous than troublesome.

Interior regions of Alaska and the Canadian Yukon are famous for periods of bitter cold winter weather. It seems logical that this season would be a challenging time to drive the Highway. Thus, I was quite surprised to learn from sourdoughs, when I first arrived in Anchorage, that they actually preferred to travel the Alaska Highway during winter! They explained patiently, "The road bed is in much better condition during the winter. There are no puddles and mud." As recently as the early to mid 1980s, long sections of the highway remained unpaved, but during winter, the frozen surface made a fine pavement so it was faster and easier to drive.

The Highway, today, is a well-used route to and from the Lower 48 and it conveys many visitors. It is cute that during summer, the vehicles on the streets of Anchorage suddenly become festooned with license plates from many other states and you can spot the most recently arrived vehicles which are also festooned with layers of dust and dried-on splashes of dirty water. In earlier years, these vehicles were even easier to spot because they arrived equipped with a handmade grid work suspended in front of their headlights and grill, to prevent rock damage. Often, spare tires and gas cans were lashed onto the roof racks.

One last tidbit … The official start of the Alaska Highway--Mile 0--is at Dawson Creek, British Columbia. The end is at Delta Junction, Alaska, Mile 1390; or, Historic Mile 1520).

Link: Milepost
www.themilepost.com

Chapter Nineteen
M/V *Columbia*

Sometimes the journey *is* the vacation.

June 23 to 29, 2007

Hi folks.

Karel and I are off on another adventure. Just now, we are on the ferry, the M/V *Columbia*. M/V, for motor vessel. We are on the second leg of a road trip that will eventually take us 28 days. We allowed two days to drive the first leg of our trip from Anchorage to Haines, where we boarded the *Columbia*. Eventually, our route home to Anchorage will take us south on the Oregon coast and Crater Lake and back toward Anchorage through northern Idaho, the Canadian Rockies, Dawson City, and the Top of the World Highway.

The *Columbia* is considered the flagship of the fleet of nine ferries in the Alaska Marine Highway. She began service in 1974 and cost nearly $20 million. The *Columbia* is 418 feet long and 85 feet wide with a gross tonnage of nearly 4,000 tons, and is driven by two 6,200 BPH diesel engines with a cruising speed of about 20 knots. She can carry over 900 passengers, plus a crew of about 60, as well as 2,700 feet of vehicles on her four deck levels. Not one 2,700-foot vehicle, of course, but the sum of the lengths of all the vehicles, which works out to about one hundred vehicles.

And it is mesmerizing to watch the amazing parade of vehicles that pour in and out of the side opening of the ferry. All but the largest vehicles that you see on the highway are part of the queue. There are no big semi-tractor trailers, of course, but almost all of the others are represented. Family sedans and vans are dwarfed by huge self-contained motor homes on their way to some adventure. Fully loaded delivery vehicles and U-Haul trucks are on their way to a remote community or on a shortcut to a new home. There is a State of

Alaska highway maintenance vehicle towing a flatbed trailer with a chunky power roller, and a smallish mud-splattered RV with a red canoe lashed on top. Several fifth-wheel motor homes and a crew-cab pickup towing an empty boat trailer. And about 20 motorcycles; one, a cherry-red tricycle towing a small, matching cherry-red trailer. Most vehicles are for travelers, but there are working vehicles, too. All enter one by one and all disembark one by one.

The M/V Columbia offloads and loads at both Haines and Skagway near the head of Chilkoot Inlet on Lynn Canal.

Some vehicles are driven into an elevator to be lifted to an upper car deck, but each is carefully positioned so there is barely enough room for a person to squeeze between and around each one. Passengers may have access to their vehicles on the lower decks for three 15-minute periods, daily, to obtain necessary items; or, most importantly, to exercise pets.

Likewise, the mix and personalities of the passengers is as varied as the vehicles that they previously inhabited. Big and small, young and old, bearded and beardless, loud and quiet. But most are courteous and happy and ready to settle in for a long ride. Each has a plan for a temporary life on the *Columbia*. Some have reserved a cabin with berths. The *Columbia* has berth space for 298 people.

Where do the other 600 people sleep? Wherever they can, and creativity reigns. First-class style is represented by the several tents that have been pitched on the two designated deck areas. These cannot be staked in place, of course, but they are fastened down with copious strips of duct tape. Other travelers planned ahead and brought an air mattress. Most have sleeping bags. Lumpy, inert figures can be spotted slumped in a chair almost any time of a day, but between 10 p.m. and 7 a.m. they really settle in and are sprawled in every convenient location. On the floors between rows of chairs and behind counters. Deck lounging chairs. Curled uncomfortably in a passenger chair. Covered by a sleeping bag, soft blanket or a space blanket. The gift shop even has make-do sleeping bags for sale. Make your cabin reservation early.

Cabins are clean, neat, functional, and compact. Ours has two bunks. (Guess who is assigned the upper one.) A toilet and a shower; a sink, a mirror and a small closet. What more could you ask for? Towels and linens? They are furnished too. One medium-sized window.

Most passengers are on board for the adventure as well as the convenience of the transportation. And make no mistake about it. This vessel is for transportation. It is not a cruise ship. The passengers are not coddled, but they are not herded, either. Stops in ports are usually brief, as little as an hour. You are expected to follow the rules, but, otherwise, you can take advantage of the many viewing opportunities from along the rail or from comfortable soft chairs through spacious, clean windows. It is not plush, but it is clean, neat, and modern. Solid. Steel. Padding. Everything is designed with function in mind. There is a very nice sit-down restaurant, a cafeteria, a cocktail bar, and several general seating areas.

The chairs on the ferry are comfortable and the there are many large windows for unobstructed viewing.

Our ride has been soft and smooth and relaxing, and, actually, usually quite entertaining. We have had little wind or wave and we are usually close to a shore or an island, protected in the Inland Passage. Occasionally, however, we did feel some swells for several half hours while crossing more exposed spaces. One person that I know of did have some queasiness. Keep your eyes on the horizon and put down your book, or go lie down.

Alaska has a longer shoreline than the rest of the United States combined and few of its coastal communities are connected with a road system. The Alaska Marine Highway System was created in 1960 as a means to connect the larger communities. Nine ferries now service the 3,500-mile system with 33 ports of call. Bellingham, Washington, on Puget Sound is the southernmost port and service areas include southeastern Alaska, Prince William Sound, southcentral Alaska and across the Gulf of Alaska to Kodiak and the Aleutian Islands. An estimated 400,000 passengers and 100,000 vehicles are transported annually.

The captain would keep the Columbia safely away from the shoreline as we cruised but he slowed for narrow or tricky passages.

Karel and I boarded in Haines, at the north end of the Lynn Canal and the upper end of the Inland Passage. We were scheduled for an 8 p.m. boarding time, but it stretched out until about 10 p.m. As so often happens in Alaska, you can schedule an event, but the schedule is really only an estimated time and the actual time will be determined by the weather, tide, and whatever else must happen first. In this case, the *Columbia* had to make a run to and from Skagway, just across the head of the fjord from Haines, with a goodly number of vehicles that were slow to load and unload. Then, we were off to Bellingham.

Skagway is only 14 miles distant from Haines, but they are quite different from each other. Both are unique compared to most of the stops along the Alaska Marine Highway because they have land highways that connect the marine highway to the rest of the world. But, although Haines has a comfortable, relaxing, lived-in personality, Skagway is a busy, bustling community that is experiencing another boom time. A gold rush of tourists, as many as 10,000 per day, who tumble out from as many as seven cruise ships at a time. Many, including Karel and me, will follow the trail of the 1898 Gold Rush Stampeders on the original White Pass Railroad. Many more will spill into the myriad of recently constructed shops, restaurants, and other tourist amenities. Some will be awed by the history and some of the original structures of the then bustling largest city in Alaska. The population in 1898 was about the same as it is today, when the cruise ships are in.

Skagway still has some original and reconstructed buildings. When a tour ship moored at the end of this main street, the number of tourists will equal or exceed the number of residents.

Finally, we are on the last full day of our trip on the *Columbia*. We are scheduled to disembark at eight in the morning at Bellingham. Karel and I are on the seventh day of our roundabout trip back to Anchorage and we have driven only two days—800 miles—before we got to Haines. While on the Columbia, we made stops in Juneau, Sitka, Petersburg, Wrangell, and Ketchikan. As it happens, several were brief and at night, but we did enjoy a daylong walking adventure in Ketchikan. We have seen perhaps 40 humpback whales, one within about 100 feet from the bow of the ferry, and we hope to see killer whales in more southerly waters. Harbor porpoises. Eagles too numerous to count. Marine birds: gulls, kittiwakes, and murreletts. Harbor seals and sea lions. I was hoping to see a bear, grizzly or black, a black-tailed deer, or a mountain goat on a shore, but that did not happen. Usually, our course challenged an easy scrutiny of a nearby shoreline but allowed an appropriate safety margin.

Views from the ferry are constantly changing with the terrain, weather, tides and time of day.

We have watched spectacular scenery ebb and flow along with the tides. It slides by at about 20 knots. The tones have changed with the daylight and the night; the sun and the clouds. Small clouds in an otherwise clear sky, tall, building puffy clouds, gray and white, low clouds and high, thin clouds. Passengers are quick with cameras–mostly digital held up and away from their eyes—and most have binoculars dangling from necks. Some track the *Columbia*'s speed and position with their own handheld GPS.

We have seen all manner of boats. Working boats: longliners, gillnetters, and purse seiners, tugs towing barges of containers, support vessels, party sportfishing boats. Pleasure boats: cruise boats, yachts, personal fishing boats, kayaks, sailboats, skiffs. And more.

We saw a wonderful assemblage of working boats in Southeastern Alaska such as this commercial salmon troller. Several baited lines or lures may be fished from each outrigger.

We would like to make this trip again, but we agree that it would be fun to stop and spend more time in the communities along the way.

If you want to ride on the Alaska State Ferry System, plan ahead. Schedule a cabin or plan your own unique sleeping arrangements. As you ride from north to south, you will have a different experience than if you ride from south to north. There is no television or radio. Limited cell phone connection, mostly near a city. No Internet. No distractions. And no gas pedal to push. Kick back and relax.

More later.

Bill and Karel

April 28, 2008

Oh, wait, there is more ... I have been lucky to live in Alaska and I have been most fortunate to be able to travel to many parts of Alaska, but most of these travels have been in South-central and Interior Alaska. As it happens, however, I have never been able to spend much time in Southeast Alaska and I have missed out on the scenery and different lifestyle of this great part of the Great Land.

Southeast Alaska makes up a small proportion of the land-mass Alaska—about 6 percent—but that land area is similar to that of the state of Indiana. Much of the land in Southeast Alaska is in islands, some very large and many small. The population was 73,000 people in 2000 and nearly half called the state capital of Juneau their home. Most of the area is covered by the Tongass National Forest, the largest in the United States. Southeastern Alaska also includes six National Parks and Monuments: Wrangell-St. Elias National Park and Preserve, Glacier Bay National Park and Preserve, Klondike Gold Rush National Historical Park, Admiralty Island National Monument, Sitka National Historical Park, and Misty Fjords National Monument.

Southeast Alaska is a temperate rain forest where the mountain slopes plunge down into the ocean. The abundant rainfall creates a lush environment for vegetative growth. Forests are dominated by huge Sitka spruce and western hemlock, but in between there are miniature forests of devil's club, ferns, berries and more. The presence of the ocean helps to temper the climate so it is relatively cool during summer and warmer in winter than in more inland areas.

Sitka black-tail deer, brown and black bears, and wolves share the forested areas and mountain goats inhabit the higher, rockier slopes, where they negotiate narrow ledges and feed on small sedges. The ocean waters are home to a variety of marine mammals, birds, and fish, including healthy populations of five species of Pacific salmon.

Historically, this region was dominated by the Tlingit people but included the Haida and Tsimshian, as well. Their culture, commerce, and subsistence were focused on the ocean and they were excellent sailors and canoe builders. The Tlingits dominated the trade routes across the coastal mountains between coastal areas and the Interior and they carved totem poles to narrate stories and document events.

Today, much of Southeast Alaska remains largely rural with several hub cities such as Juneau, Sitka, Ketchikan, and Wrangell, but there are many small communities such as Elfin Cove, Hyder, Tenakee Springs, and Baranof Warm Springs. The predominant sources of income include commercial fishing, tourism, and government. Logging was an important industry, but it has waned.

People living in Southeast Alaska today, much like the earlier inhabitants of the region, continue to enjoy the bounty supplied by the forests and the ocean. Hunting for black-tailed deer and mountain goats is a popular activity. Fresh fish are readily available. The favorites are halibut and salmon. Trolling for Chinook salmon is popular and the annual Juneau salmon derby is a fun event.

Sitka was the site of the first non-native settlement in Southeast Alaska. Russian fur traders established an outpost there in 1741. Sitka was also the site where Russia officially transferred Alaska to the United States in 1867 and it remained the capital of the Territory of Alaska until 1906.

Although Juneau is the capital of the state, it is not accessible by road. Access is only by aircraft or by boat. In the 1970s state residents voted to move the state capital to Willow, about two hours north of Anchorage, but eventually, the momentum waned and Juneau continues to be the capital. Juneau is at sea level, but the adjacent mountains are capped by the Juneau Icefield which feeds a number of glaciers, including the Mendenhall Glacier. The Mendenhall glacier is a large glacier that is readily accessible from the Juneau road system.

One last tidbit … At the time of Statehood in 1959, one proposal was to create two states; one of which was Southeastern Alaska.

Link: Alaska Marine Highway
http://www.dot.state.ak.us/amhs/index.shtml

Section Five—Work Alaska

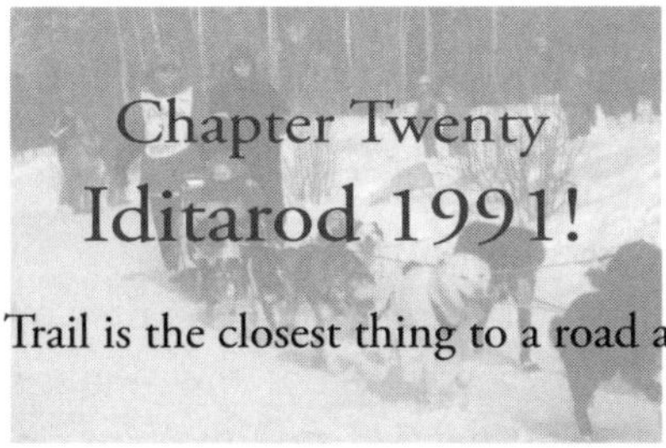

Chapter Twenty
Iditarod 1991!

The Iditarod Trail is the closest thing to a road across Alaska.

March 4, 1991

Hello.

This is bizarre. I really don't believe that this is happening. As I write this, I am sitting in the Nome airport. I am listening to a radio and I hope to get at least one more good Iditarod update before I board my plane. Right now, the plane is late, but they just announced that the plane could not land in Kotzebue because of weather conditions, so it will be here soon.

The first musher may cross the finish line within hours. A chance of a lifetime. I could see the finish of the Iditarod sled dog race and the winner should be Rick Swenson.

You know what. Somehow it really doesn't bother me. It would be exciting to see the winner, but I am comfortable with this situation.

Actually, in the past 3 days I have become just about maxed out with things Iditarod and I have seen and experienced more of the Iditarod than any ordinary person can expect. Today, I functioned as a de-facto trailbreaker between Nome and the Safety Roadhouse, which is the last Iditarod checkpoint before Nome. Four of us ran from Nome to Safety Roadhouse on snowmachines, spent about an hour waiting for weather to improve. It did not so we just returned to Nome.

A radio report: Minus 70 degree Fahrenheit wind chill on the trail. More radio: Swenson is still *not* into Safety Roadhouse. Earlier, I had heard that he *was* into Safety. Rumors, forecasts, predictions, and what-ifs have been rampant in Nome.

You might ask, what's going on? Why am I here? Would you believe? I'm here on business. This *is* a business trip. I just happen to be in Nome and it just happens that the first Iditarod finisher is coming in. I arrived on Tuesday to visit a small fish hatchery project at the Nome High School and to examine several sites as possible locations for streamside salmon egg incubator projects.

Another radio report: How dramatic a bit of information can be! Mushers are pinned down all along the trail. Most are at checkpoints. At least six are in places unknown. Wind, ground blizzards, snow. All over. There has been virtually no news. And no changes all day. The previous report had said that Susan Butcher led Rick Swenson out of the White Mountain checkpoint by an hour as she said "Nothing will stop me now." She was on her way to the Safety checkpoint and only 77 miles to go to the finish line in Nome. It should be an eight-hour trip with a one-hour head start. That was at 7:30 last night. Martin Buser, Lavon Barve, and Joe Runyan also hit the trail as soon as they could. No way could they catch her.

But she returned to White Mountain after 1½ hours! So did Runyan and others. Swenson and Buser were not seen. In an eight-hour run, they have been unseen for 15 to 18 hours. Were they lost? Were they safe? Whiteout conditions with 30- to 50-mile-per-hour winds. This section of the trail was the most difficult. Where are they? We fear the worst. So far, by luck, there has never been a fatality on the trail. *And*, what about all those other mushers farther back on the trail?

While we were at the Safety Roadhouse, two trailbreakers started toward White Mountain on snowmachines. Conditions were horrid. Before long, they decided to turn back, so they picked out a trail marker as a center point and turned around it to return. Trail markers are located about 30 to 50 yards apart. But they *got lost*! They couldn't see another marker. Luckily, they were eventually able find their way back to Safety.

Oh! Some news! Now Rick has been spotted. Only about 10 miles out of Safety, just on this side of Topcock Rock. The worst part of the trail and the worst weather is behind him. In an hour, he will be into Safety; then, in less than three hours he will be in Nome.

The pilot just came onto the loudspeaker. Our plane will go back to Kotzebue and try to land; then come back to pick us up. More delay. I hope you won't mind a long letter. Actually, maybe this plane won't even be able to land here when it returns. I sure wouldn't mind seeing Rick come across the finish line.

Anyhow, yesterday I went on my first snowmachine ride ever. I was traveling with Charlie and Pete, who were also fish biologists. Basically, we were looking for open-water areas where fish could survive through the winter and sites that could be developed to incubate large numbers of fish eggs. During recent years, the numbers of returning salmon have been dwindling in the streams around Nome and we were investigating ways to increase the population numbers. Open water in February is an indicator of upwelling groundwater, which is relatively warm. Such a site could possibly be used to operate a salmon egg incubation box.

When conditions are good you can cover a lot of ground very fast on snowmachines. Open water in winter is an indicator of groundwater and is a good candidate location for installing salmon egg incubation boxes. (ADF&G Photo)

Two insulated egg-incubation boxes. Water is collected at an upstream location and piped to the egg box where it percolates up through a substrate that has been seeded with fertilized salmon eggs. (ADF&G Photo)

It was a gorgeous day! Bright and clear, but cold. Minus 6 degrees Fahrenheit when we started. Not much wind, but snowmobiles are fast and create their own wind chill. After 10 minutes or so, I started to feel comfortable enough to relax and enjoy the ride, but by then we had gone through the most fun part of the trip when we scooted down a gully that felt like a slalom course. Later, it wasn't fun at all when we traversed around a hill that was crusted in an icy shell. I hung out as far to one side as possible to counterbalance so the machine would not side-slip and roll down into the stream bottom 300 feet below. What? Oh no! Then I learned that we would have to return over the same route! Some project sites looked promising. Beautiful trip. We saw some ptarmigan and some moose.

Today, we had intended to check out a side drainage of the Solomon River, 8 miles past the Safety Roadhouse; then we would go up the drainage 6 miles. It was a much flatter and much more open trip, along the coast of Norton Sound east of Nome. About minus 5 or 6 degrees Fahrenheit again; light snow, but pleasant in Nome. Within minutes, we were at the edge of Norton Sound on the Bering Sea. Winds were probably 15 to 25 miles per hour. We were tightly bundled but it was about an hour trip to Safety. My biggest problem was breathing through my face mask. The moisture in my breath froze in the cold air as we traveled at 20 to 35 miles per hour and I got a bit of frostbite on my left cheek before I relearned how to breathe through that mask without causing condensation.

Finally, I am on the plane and we are on the runway. We are off to Kotzebue.

You know, of course, that we didn't make it past the Safety Roadhouse. This was a wise decision and it also gave us an extra 2 hours back in Nome for us to review our observations and lay out some plans. Rick Swenson's father and about 15 other people were waiting in the Safety Roadhouse. And waiting. No news. Then, a radio report! Missing mushers. No new news. The weather seems to be improving–or maybe it's getting worse. We hoped, at least, that everyone was safe. We hoped Rick could pull it off. Last year at Safety his dogs mutinied; they just quit. They forced him to a stop. Maybe this will be his year.

This has been a marvelous experience. It could only have been better if a musher had come through while we were at the Safety checkpoint, especially if it was Rick or Martin. That would have been more exciting than to see a finisher in Nome. Of course, I'd like to see the finishing of an Iditarod. Who wouldn't? But I'm comfortable. I've already seen and experienced more than I could ever hope for.

Oh, and I ran into another coworker in Nome, Peter, who works in Kotzebue with Kate, an Iditarod musher. Kate has maintained a lead as the top rookie in this race. So I had another special interest in following this race. Peter and I made morning and evening pilgrimages to the Nome Iditarod Race Headquarters to check on her progress along with the rest of the mushers. He phoned her parents in Iowa City to keep them up to date. The last I heard, she had arrived at Koyuk along with ten or twelve other racers. One or two have left and no one knows where they are. She's been stuck there for a day. How much longer? The trail will be bad when they leave. Deep snow, soft.

There will be no trail until the villagers start to move around on their "snow go's." The mushers will have to work together to break trail. Then what?

The first day of the Iditarod Race is not counted; instead, it is an exuberant ceremonial start from downtown Anchorage and winds about 15 miles through the city. The sled hauls a rider who has bid for the opportunity and the mushers have a dog handler trailing behind on another sled. Note that some dogs wear a jacket and most dogs are wearing protective booties.

Right now, it looks as if Rick should take first. Where is Martin Buser? Holed up in a cabin between White Mountain and Safety, we hope. Once they start to move, there should be a hellacious race for the next five places. And the next five after that. How long will it take for the weather to break? It seems to be improving. Then what will happen?

We are over Kotzebue now, looking for a hole in the weather so we can land. I just want to get home. And so do the mushers, I'm sure.

In Nome, it was fun to see the activity. And the people. Oh, I didn't tell you. I actually did meet the first musher who arrived in Nome. It was Libby Riddles (that was *her* joke; she didn't race this year) and I got her autograph for Donna. Donna wanted me to get DeeDee Jonrowe's autograph when she won this year but DeeDee is pinned down with Kate in Koyuk.

Late Tuesday evening, the race committee in Nome set up snow fences to mark the finish chute. The big burl arch was already in place when I arrived. They began to spread snow on the main street for the finishers. Every two or three hours, a newly updated printout was posted that listed all the mushers.

Pins with name tags are moved on a big map. Few were actually moved while I was in Nome. I attended the press briefing on Wednesday night. That was when Susan had an hour's lead on Rick and was expected into Nome as early as eight or nine o'clock this morning. They outlined the schedule of events for the finish and the big sponsor, of course, had the priority for the interviews. I passed up the wet-Tee-shirt contest on Tuesday evening and the wet-buns contest (for men) the next night at the same bar. Lots of tourists. Many people, just waiting. The locals were nonchalant. They had jobs to do and tried to get their work done, but they also were curious to hear each update.

The finish line of the Last Great Race is in midtown Nome on the main street beside Norton Sound. Lance Mackey won the 1,149-mile for the third time in 2009 with a time of nine days and 21 hours. The last-place musher was on the trail for 15 days and 14 hours.

We've given up on landing in Kotzebue and finally, we are on our way to Anchorage. If I'm lucky, I'll see a live broadcast on TV of Rick Swenson crossing the finish line in Nome.

Say; have you ever wondered how the mushers were able to keep track of their racing bibs through those 1,100 to 1,200 miles of trail? Simple, they don't. They were all neatly stacked, clean and white, in Safety Roadhouse. Someone was carefully watching to be sure nothing got stacked on top of them so they would be ready at a moments notice so the musher would waste no time putting it on during the check-in, and so they would look good when they arrived in Nome.

Well, this was a wonderful trip. I certainly have a new and different appreciation for snowmachines (they are not so bad, after all, especially as transportation) and dog mushing. I think I had a special, vicarious trail-situation experience with the feel of the wind and the limiting view of a wind-blown trail. And the sense of awareness and concern of so many people along the way. The waiting, the uncertainty, and the hazards.

I'm home. Good news! Martin Buser has shown up at the Safety checkpoint. Buser got separated from his team, but he had walked to a checkpoint and later found his dogs. Meanwhile, Rick left Safety before Buser and is expected at Nome before too long.

I feel very good. My cheek is still sore; so is my right big toe that got cold. My fingers are a little stiff from holding onto the handle bars and my thumb from working the throttle. My thighs are sore from straddling the seat. Shoulders are stiff too. We covered nearly 100 miles on snowmachines in two days.

I chatted with some volunteer veterinarians during the flight. They were from France; they had been at the Rhon Roadhouse and another checkpoint; now they were heading home, too. I also met three Eskimos who reminded me that Nome got its name because an early handwritten map marked a nearby spot "?Name." This morphed into "C. Nome" and "Cape Nome" and the town became "Nome."

It's 1:25 a.m. According to the radio, Rick is nearly in. Now it is on the television. I recognize the buildings. He is in! The winner. The beginning of the end. Still 65 or so more mushers to go. He is really frosted up. Buser is on the way, maybe an hour out.

It's been a long day… longer for the mushers. To bed for me. Tomorrow I go back to work in my office.

Good night. Love.

Bill

February 26, 2007

Oh, wait, there is more … the Iditarod race caught my attention from the very first year I came to Anchorage. Although the first race was held in 1973, various parts of the Iditarod Trail had been used by gold miners since the early 1900s. Travel by dogsled was the only reliable form of transportation during winters and mail delivery depended on the dogs. When the tundra was frozen and snow covered, dog team drivers could move overland with ease so mail and freight were hauled from the ports of Seward and Nome inland to the goldfields. The trail took its name from the town of Iditarod which, in its heyday, was the largest town in Alaska with 10,000 inhabitants. Eventually, the bust overran the boom and Iditarod became a ghost town. Snowmachines and airplanes changed how people traveled, which caused dog teams to begin to disappear. By the 1960s, the Iditarod Trail had become largely forgotten and overgrown by brush in some areas, but Dorothy Page and Joe Redington evolved the idea of restoring the trail and holding a dog race to revive the sport.

Dog mushing gained a flash of notoriety in 1925 when diphtheria broke out in Nome. Serum was in Anchorage and no pilot was available to fly it to Nome. Instead, it was loaded on a train and sent on the Alaska Railroad to Nenana, where it was transferred to a dogsled that took it in relays from village to village down the Tanana and Yukon rivers to the crossing to Norton Sound and into Nome.

The present-day Iditarod Trail begins in Seward and ends in Nome. Officially, the race, which begins in Anchorage, is 1,149 miles long. The 49 is for the 49th state, Alaska. Actually, the exact distance is somewhat uncertain because there is no one clear-cut path and it is somewhat different each year depending on where the track is actually set and marked. The race includes a ceremonial start in Anchorage followed on the next day by the official restart in Wasilla, the official home of the Iditarod, or Willow, depending on snow conditions. All decisions are based on the well-being of the dogs.

The Iditarod race has changed greatly over the years. The first race was won in just over twenty days. The winning time today is between nine and 12 days. There were 34 mushers in the first race with 22 finishers. A total of 83 mushers are scheduled to start in 2007; including eight from countries other than the United States. Twenty-seven will be on the trail as rookies, but even rookies are required to have prior long-distance sled dog racing experience.

Why is the Iditarod race such a challenge? Because it is so unpredictable. Mushers come from all over the world and each trains with his or her dogs under a particular set of conditions. Very cold or balmy. Heavy snow or sparse. Some will be well trained for the actual trail conditions, but conditions will be different over the length of the trail and they may change during the 10 or more days on the trail. Consider the logistical challenge of flying dog and human food and supplies into each of the 26 or 27 checkpoints by volunteer pilots. Frozen rivers are excellent highways–unless they are windswept with glare ice or covered with overflow, which happens when the ice releases and a layer of liquid water forms over the ice. No matter what, dogs must be fed, watered, and rested before the driver eats or rests.

You can imagine the physical and economic cost to maintain a kennel and run the race.

There is more, too. In addition to routine transportation by snowmachines and dog sledders, the Iditarod Trail is used for the first half of the 2,000-mile Iron Dog snowmachine race from Anchorage to Nome to Fairbanks. The fastest racers finish in less than 40 hours and average over 50 miles an hour. Portions of the trail are used for the Junior Iditarod and the Alaska Ultra Sport 350 and 1,100-mile midwinter "human-powered" race. The Yukon Quest is another challenging long-distance sled dog race between Fairbanks and Whitehorse in Canada. Other long distance and shorter sprint sled dog races are also staged in many parts of Alaska.

All in all, it is great fun to follow the race and live vicariously with the mushers, but I have been fortunate, over the years, to personally know and cheer individual mushers in the race. That makes it even more fun.

One last tidbit… dog mushing is the official sport of Alaska.

Link: Iditarod web site
http://www.iditarod.com/

Iditarod National Historic Trail
http://www.blm.gov/ak/iditarod/

Chapter Twenty-One
Looking for Chums

Chum salmon are important fish for the Yukon River fisheries.

October 10, 1994

Hello all.

I have time to write another letter. I hope that you don't get too bored with these and I hope you are all feeling fine.

Right now, I am feeling fine, too, but I know that I have a lot of work to do before I will be ready to leave this field camp. Right now, I am relaxing in a tent. I am lying on a cot with a soft padding, on top of my sleeping bag. It is toasty warm in here. We actually have a propane heater to keep things warm and a Coleman lantern, too, that throws a lot of heat. Outside, it is about 25 degrees Fahrenheit. The night is clear and the northern lights are glowing and flowing. I want to do some writing, but I am tired and I do want to watch the aurora some more, too. Earlier, while I was in the outhouse, I could watch them through the open door.

Okay, where am I this time? I am on the Toklat River, just north of the Denali National Park boundary, about 60 miles downstream from the park road. The Toklat River drains north from the park into the Kantishna River before it enters the Tanana River on its way downstream to the Yukon River.

Why am I here? I am the project leader for a small research project to evaluate the quality and quantity of the spawning habitat for an important population of chum salmon.

This is my second night here, so I am just getting started. Not much to say just yet except that there are *lots* of chum salmon. Today was a beautiful day. Early on, we had a great view of Mount McKinley. That mountain is so big. We saw some swans, a few eagles and two sets of grizzly bear tracks.

It was easy to find a good flat spot for our big comfortable camp on the broad glacial floodplain of the Toklat River. (ADF&G Photo)

Today was another long day. It is hard to get started early because it just feels too cold. Then we get rolling and don't seem to finish up until dark. Daylight is from about eight o'clock in the morning until seven o'clock in the evening. Today was another nice day but with high overcast, no wind, and the high temperature was about 32 degrees Fahrenheit.

The weather was crisp and clear, and it was exciting just to be able to take in the landscape.

Early today, I helped the crew from a nearby fish hatchery take about 200,000 eggs from the chum salmon that were concentrated below their weir, and before the eggs were airlifted to the hatchery, I went with Betsy and Jim on an aerial reconnaissance by helicopter over part of the area that we will cover with our survey. We determined that one section would be very difficult to manage from the ground because of deep snow and downed trees; and, perhaps, low priority as well. I concluded that we could get enough data from aerial photos.

Here is what we did. I took the copilot seat in the two-person helicopter. The side door was removed and I was strapped in so I could lean out and shoot photos nearly straight down from 320 feet above the ground. I think it worked quite well, but won't know for sure until the film is processed. I shot more than 72 frames as the pilot moved slowly upstream. When I needed to change the roll of film, he just stopped and simply hovered in place.

During winter, this area was accessible only by snowmachine or helicopter. (ADF&G Photo)

Actually, it almost seems that we have a small town here. Jim and Dave came in last week to set up camp and prepare for the egg take. They also work for the Alaska Department of Fish and Game. Tim and Dave O., who work for a Native organization, arrived a day later to begin their research project. Betsy and I came for our work. Now, Dave has finished his tasks and flew out with the load of fish eggs. Jim is still here to help Betsy and me. Meanwhile, more Department employees have arrived. Dave S. came in today to take tissue samples from the salmon for genetic analyses. Two other people also came in today to get a count of the numbers of spawning fish. All travel is by helicopter. The nearest road access is 30 miles away.

So why all this interest in the Toklat River chum salmon? Historically, the Toklat River has been an important producer of chum salmon for the Yukon River fishery. In the most recent 10 to 15 years, however, the production has been far below expectations and we are trying to learn why. My job is to focus on the spawning habitat. Betsy is my field team leader and together, we are working out methods and priorities for the studies. When she is comfortable with the plan, I will catch a ride out and she and Jim will finish up.

Why is this place so special to the fish? Because chum salmon in this part of Alaska spawn in areas where relatively warm water, about 40 degrees Fahrenheit, flows up, spring-like, through the gravel. The flowing water is important, of course, to bring oxygen to the developing embryos and the warm groundwater incubates the embryos so they hatch and emerge at the correct time in the spring. This area has lots of warm upwelling groundwater. We need to measure the amount of this area to estimate how many fish may be able to spawn here.

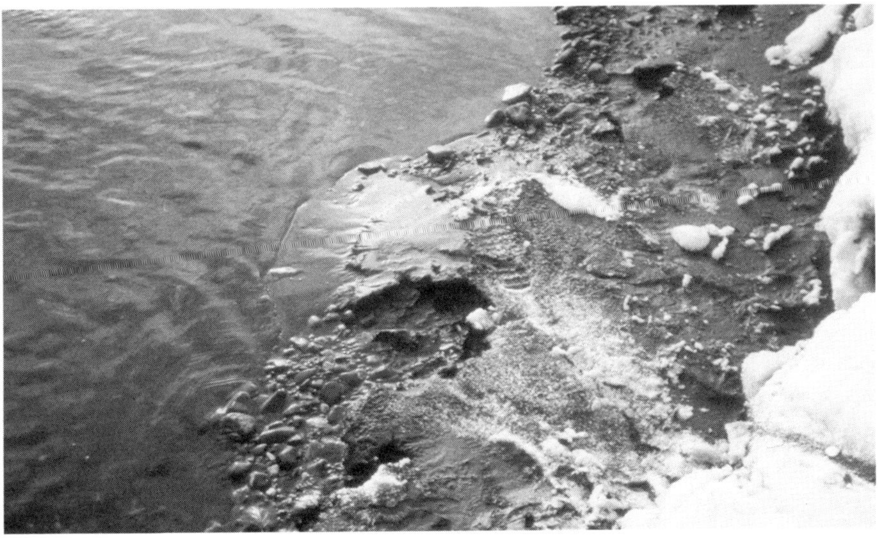

Streams, ponds, and rivers were freezing up, but these braids of the Toklat River were ice free because of the springs and upwelling areas that were around 40°F. (ADF&G Photo)

I'd best stop, it is time to hit the sack. It will be another full day tomorrow. It is really comfortable in the tent now. Almost too warm.

October 14

Well, we didn't see a grizzly bear today. I guess that's all right. I would like to see one and they are nearby, but unfortunately, they are the ones who usually get to choose the time and place to see and be seen. Today, we were in the right time and place, but they did not choose. And that's okay.

Our job is to measure the area of spawning habitat. That means that we get to look at lots of spawning chum salmon splashing around in very shallow water. One of the areas that we measured today not only had lots of spawning chum salmon, but also lots of fish along the shore with bite marks in them. It snowed last night. This area was all beaten down by noon today with bear tracks and big round bear butt marks where they sat. None of the tracks were huge; some were small and cute—only four or five inches across—so at least some of the bears were sows with cubs. Many of the fish had only one or several round holes in them so they were merely caught and tossed aside. Some had only one bite missing, some lay there with fresh, unfrozen blood. The bears were close, but they chose to stay out of sight.

This is really a beautiful area. I am lucky to be able to experience this part of Alaska. Jim often spends much of his winters here trapping for marten, occasionally wolf or beaver. Oh, that reminds me, today we also saw fresh wolf tracks. I can only imagine how wonderful and peaceful it is on a clear winter night here alone with the northern lights flaring. I am sure, too, that the 30-mile snowmachine ride to get here can also be a challenge at times. And sometimes, Jim traps as far as 40 to 50 miles beyond here.

October 15

Good morning. How are you this morning? I've just crawled back into my sleeping bag. I thought that Jim was up, but after I got dressed, I discovered that there was no light next door so I decided not to disturb him. It is still dark and chilly but we expect to have good weather today to get as much work done that we can.

This is a very comfortable camp. The main tent is a 12-by- 14-foot wall tent on a wooden frame. It has a good woodstove and a small table for a 3-burner cook stove, two cots, and another table. There is a six-person sleeping tent with two cots, two small tables, and a propane heater that we use early and late in the day. There is another smaller wall tent with two cots, a woodstove and a cooking and storage area. One more tent is just for storage. We are cool at times, but very comfy.

Betsy and Jim are great working companions. And Tim and Paul are great associates, too. They are focused on their own aspect of the research, but we share results from our daily experiences. Jim has such an intimate knowledge of the area and he has wonderful ideas and can solve every problem. Betsy likes to understand just what task we need to accomplish and then she goes ahead and gets it done.

Well, I may be leaving tomorrow. Jim and Betsy still have several days of work to finish up, and then close down the camp, and leave. I feel sad to leave. It has been a great week here and a wonderful experience. Besides, I feel that we are a good team and I feel that I am letting them down. I know that they will be able to do the job; that is not a problem at all. It will be hard to say goodbye, but weather permitting I will be riding a helicopter back to Fairbanks tomorrow.

We sure did a lot of walking yesterday and today. We covered a lot of ground. The whole area is about a mile wide and as much as four miles long. Braids of channels and sloughs with spawning habitat wind back and forth throughout this glacial floodplain. Lots of fish. Lots of pretty water. Lots of walking to cover it all.

Good food in this camp! Rib steaks, ham, bacon and eggs, pork cutlets; one day, Jim slow-roasted two wild mallard ducks that he had shot. It took three to four hours in the Dutch oven. And were they good! Biscuits in a camp oven. Spaghetti. A stew is next on the list. Chicken, too. Excellent.

October 16

Wow. Another abrupt transition. About two hours ago, I boarded a helicopter at a small camp on the edge of the Toklat River. Thirty minutes later, I was in Fairbanks. Another 30 or 45 minutes, and I am on airplane to Anchorage. It will be nice to be home, but the Toklat River will always be a special place for me.

Chum salmon are sometimes called dog salmon. Two reasons: the mature males develop big, strong teeth that resemble the canine teeth of dogs, and chum salmon have traditionally been used as dog food, either dried or frozen. In fact, near where we were camped, there is an old roadhouse that was built in the early 1900s to service travelers and assist mail delivery to the nearby mining camps. The easiest way to travel across the tundra and forest is by dogsled in the winter. The spawning fish were netted, frozen or dried and stored to feed the sled dog teams. Although many travelers today use snow-machines, dog teams are still being used and chum salmon are harvested for commercial sale, human subsistence use, and dog food.

The relatively warm, upwelling ground water in the braids provided excellent conditions for the late-spawning population of chum salmon. In the early 1900s, the operator of a nearby roadhouse harvested the chum salmon as feed for the sled dog teams that hauled the mail. (ADF&G Photo)

I will be looking forward to evaluating the data and information we are collecting. Actually, this part of the study will not be complete until March, but I expect that there will be a second year of studies, too. Betsy and Jim are installing a series of monitors to determine if some of the spawning areas freeze out during the winter. It is not enough for a fish to spawn successfully unless the eggs survive to hatching and the young fish can begin their journey to the ocean to repeat the cycle.

I am nearly home so I will be closing down here soon. I have enjoyed sharing these thoughts and a snippet of my experience on the Toklat River. I hope you enjoyed it, too.

Winter is closing in now on Alaska. In fact, last night was our first significant snowfall in the vicinity of Fairbanks and the Toklat River. I really did not expect to get out of the camp today. Conditions improved just enough for just long enough for the pilot to make one round-trip. The rivers are flowing with slush ice and ice floes. Anchor ice is beginning to form on the bottom. Water temperatures in the rivers are about minus 0.5 degrees Celsius or 30 degrees Fahrenheit. It was warm while I was out, but never above freezing. The weather forecast is predicting zero degrees Fahrenheit for Fairbanks for tomorrow. I am wondering what it will be like in Anchorage.

8:00 p.m.

I am home again. I am thinking about Jim and Betsy and wondering how cold it is on the Toklat River and how much snow fell there today. Here, we have nearly four inches, but it is thick and sticky compared to the soft dry snow we had by the river.

I am happy to be back with my family, but now I think back to the time I spent on the Toklat River. I am pleased that I was able to do my share of the field work. As an old chair-bound fish biologist, I am pleased that I am not too sore and stiff. Time to quit.

Till later, *Bill*

February 8, 2009

Oh, wait, there is more … Salmon grow and mature in the ocean and return to freshwater to spawn. And after they enter freshwater, salmon stop feeding. They do bite on things, but they do not ingest anything. You have probably heard this before but have you ever wondered what they live on during this time? If they do not eat, what do they have to metabolize for the energy they need to swim upstream and go through a courtship and spawning?

Ironically, salmon rely on the same energy source to migrate as we do. Oil. Of course, salmon and petrochemical oil that we use do not mix well. The oil that the salmon use is their own natural oil or body fat, called lipids.

Salmon accumulate lipids during their oceanic migration. It is their job to eat. They eat for survival. They eat to grow and mature. And they eat to accumulate and store fat as fuel for their freshwater migration to the spawning grounds. There is no more feeding. They need to have enough fuel in their tank to burn for energy during the migration, nest guarding and building, and spawning. Their fuel tank is mainly their muscles and around the intestines where the fat is stored. The muscle, itself, is also partially metabolized, but most of the energy is from the oil

But here is where things begin to get interesting. Each species and each spawning stock is adapted for their particular spawning site. The entire spawning process may take as much as 15 days and death ensues in about a week after that. But the duration and difficulty of the migration is highly variable. Pink salmon usually spawn close to the head of the tide so they do not need so much fuel. Some chinook and chum salmon stocks, however, migrate nearly 2,000 miles or more up the Yukon River into Canada before they spawn. Some are traveling at a rate of about 50 miles per day. Those salmon need some pretty large fuel tanks.

Chum salmon stocks with short spawning migrations have an average composition of about 4 percent fat. Chum salmon stocks, however, that migrate far up the Yukon River have an average of about 14 percent fat. Some upstream stocks of Chinook salmon reportedly start their spawning migration with 24 to 30 percent fat content—some reports are even higher—more than any other known stock of salmon.

As salmon migrate farther upstream and as they progress through the spawning process, their body composition changes. Fat and protein are progressively used up and it is progressively replaced by water. By the time of death, salmon have depleted almost all of their fat and nearly half of their protein.

What does all this mean to you and me? First, many people rate salmon with the highest fat content as the most flavorful.

Guess what. Many people consider upstream spawning stocks of Yukon River Chinook salmon among the tastiest of all salmon. Yukon River chum salmon are also savored. These fishes command a high price in fish markets, particularly in Japan. In addition, roe from these stocks is considered the best for salmon egg caviar and for sushi.

Pink salmon stocks, on the other hand, generally exhibit among the lowest of concentrations of fat in their bodies. This, in part, explains why they are less popular for eating. Some Native groups, however, have a preference for pink salmon, including spawning pink salmon, because they are easier to dry and preserve for later use.

Stored oil is important for salmon as fuel for migration, but it is also extremely important in another way. Female salmon must accumulate oil as fuel for migration, but also to store in their eggs as fuel for metabolism for the developing embryo. The unfertilized egg is little more than a tiny globe filled with fish oil. The fertilized egg incubates and the embryo utilizes the oil for energy. Upon hatching, the remaining oil is trapped in the yolk sac, which the alevin uses while still buried in the gravel of the redd. After the alevin has used up the yolk sac, it migrates up and out of the redd to become a free-swimming fry. These fry are now on their own and must find their own food.

It really does not stop here. After the spawning salmon have given up their energy for migration, spawning, egg and fry development, and death, they keep on giving. Their carcasses deteriorate and the breakdown products are released into the streams, lakes, and rivers to fertilize the base of the food chain to enhance the opportunity of survival for the next generation.

We all need energy. We all need fuel for energy. We need fuel for movement and other activities. But if you think about it, a salmon body is much like a self-propelled fuel tank that is used to transport eggs or sperm and fertilizer up a stream from the ocean.

One last tidbit. Chum salmon are often called dog salmon, but in the fish stores, they are often labeled as silverbrite or keta salmon. Keta is the scientific species name for chum salmon.

Link: Learn more about the Yukon River
at the Yukon River Drainage Fisheries Association
http://www.yukonsalmon.org/index.htm

Chapter Twenty-Two
Work—Alaska Style

A brief, but awesome, view of wonderful Alaska scenery.

October 24, 1992

Hello again!

I know that I wrote recently, but I was on a trip just yesterday and I saw some awesome scenery that I need to share with you.

I was asked to go to Homer to help with a bit of field work. It had originally been scheduled for two days ago, but because we needed to fly out to a remote site, we needed decent flying weather. At 9 a.m., the trip was postponed because it was too cloudy to safely fly out to our destination. Yesterday, it was a go.

Mark met me at the Homer Airport and after a brief stop at the Fish and Game office, we hurried to the helicopter pad. This trip was by helicopter because the local lakes had frozen up a week ago and floatplanes could not operate. As usual, we were on Alaska Bush Time. The helicopter was out on a job that took longer than expected so we had to wait and we got a late start.

The purpose of our trip was to install a short perforated pipe vertically in the streambed to measure changes in the groundwater level during the winter in an old side channel of Port Dick Creek. With these and other data, we can make plans to develop a spawning channel to create more spawning habitat for chum salmon. We drove the pipe with a sledgehammer and we pulled on it with pipe wrenches. One thing I did learn is that these fingers are better adapted to holding pencils and typing on a keyboard than for pounding and plumbing.

Anyhow, I have had some limited flying time in a helicopter, but this flight was wonderfully dramatic. We softly and gently lifted off. There was no sound inside my earphones. We floated over the edge of the airport and paralleled the Homer Spit out, over, and across Kachemak Bay. The tide was very high.

There was no wind. The water was very flat. The air was perfect! There were no clouds. The sun was bright. It was absolutely gorgeous! The sky was a bright, brilliant blue. The water was a dark, deep blue with a tinge of green. There was no limit to our visibility. The view from our helicopter was nearly unrestricted. There was a narrow post or two, but the floor was narrow and the window bubbled out. The cockpit was designed for good viewing.

After the tributary of Port Dick Creek was reconstructed, it had good quantity and quality of water for salmon spawning. (ADF&G Photo)

The shoreline reaches out with brown fingers into the bay. Behind, the brown turns into tall, blue-black spruce trees. Suddenly, we are over snow! New, bright and clean. Brilliant white in the sun with shadows of blue. We follow gently up the edge of a glacier. Suddenly, we are among the peaks and we are on the other side. There! A mountain goat!

The helicopter landed us and our gear near the mouth of Port Dick Creek at low tide. (ADF&G Photo)

The pilot maneuvered along the shoreline and gently lowered us into a small open area right at the head of the tide in the Port Dick Estuary. The scenery was magnificent.

Fresh snow coats the mountain peaks and a glacier on the lower Kenai Peninsula on a spectacularly bright and clear day.

We did our work and met our pickup ride, right on schedule. We returned by a slightly different route. There was no glacier here, but we hovered even lower. Once, we were in a deep gorge seemingly only a hundred feet above the trees and with a hundred feet of clearance on each side.

The east side of Kachemak Bay is rimmed with islands, lagoons, bays and spits of land.

We flew directly toward a steep cliff, but the helicopter flowed up, over, and back down as if we were protected by a force field. A few sea otters and a cluster of sea lions attracted our attention as we flew on. The pilot's voice came through the headphones. "It's days like these that I just *love* flying a helicopter."

We are back over Homer Spit. Then, the touchdown is so gentle that you hardly know the flight is over.

It is days like these that make living in Alaska so special—even if my fingers are made for office work. See you!

Love. *Bill*

February 26, 2007

Oh, wait, there is more ... This brief letter is about the spectacular scenery that surrounds Kachemak Bay and a most unique way to experience it, but there is much more to say about the work that we were doing that made it all possible. Our work task was to set up monitoring equipment to evaluate the depth of groundwater and whether it might freeze during winter. The goal of the project was to create or reestablish spawning habitat for chum salmon.

This work site was located in an old streambed on the south side of the Kenai Peninsula at the head of the West Arm Port Dick Bay, which opens to the Gulf of Alaska. The stream, Port Dick Creek, did at one time sustain a run of chum salmon, but some years prior, a small landslide filled the streambed with gravel and we suspected that the water still flowed below the surface.

All salmon and trout require moving, well-oxygenated freshwater for spawning and successful hatching of eggs. The water supply must be continuous and the eggs cannot freeze. But each of the five species of North American Pacific salmon prefer to spawn in different parts of a drainage and each has different requirements for successful rearing of the juvenile life stage.

The five species of Pacific salmon in North America are:

Chum salmon; commonly called, dog salmon or silverbrites

Pink salmon; commonly called, humpbacked salmon or humpies

Sockeye salmon; commonly called, red salmon

Chinook salmon; commonly called, king salmon

Coho salmon; commonly called, silver salmon

Of these, chum salmon are well suited for the type of spawning habitat that we expected to create because they prefer to spawn in places where the groundwater flows or upwells from the bottom of streams. Pink salmon are less fussy about where they like to spawn, from the head of tide to middle reaches of streams. Sockeye salmon also usually spawn in streams and rivers; but, usually where there is a lake nearby. Chinook salmon usually spawn in the larger streams and rivers, usually in the middle and upper reaches. Coho salmon usually spawn in the small, uppermost reaches of streams. (Sorry for the overuse of the word *usually*, but there are just too many special adaptations by the many separate populations; so, there are no hard and fast rules.)

In addition, pink and chum salmon have the least requirement for freshwater. After the eggs are deposited in the gravel, the fry hatch, and in late spring the young fish work their way up out of the gravel nest, called a redd, and into the moving water. Then, they keep going directly to the ocean, where they begin to feed on the small plankton organisms. There is no rearing in freshwater; however, the young life stages of sockeye, Chinook, and coho salmon, depend on one or more years of rearing in freshwater. Sockeye salmon fry feed on small freshwater plankton in lakes for one to three years before they migrate to the ocean. Young Chinook salmon prefer to rear along the streambanks of rivers for a year before migrating and small coho salmon usually spend two or more years in the small streams and slough habitat such as beaver ponds before they migrate.

So we expected that the spawning habitat Port Dick Creek would be well suited for chum salmon, but we expected that some pink salmon would spawn there as well. There were no lakes in the drainage where sockeye salmon might rear, and rearing habitat for Chinook and coho salmon was limited, so we assumed that few, if any might be found here.

This is not a simple process. It requires planning and funding. And we can only hope that the fish will respond as we predict. After several years of research and more field work, the streambed was developed, the excess gravel was removed, and the project was successful. The spawning habitat was redeveloped and a good run of chum salmon was reestablished.

I just learned, I am afraid to say, that several years of good returns were followed by two or more years of bad flooding and the redeveloped spawning habitat was buried again by several feet of gravel. Mother Nature is not a nice player.

One last tidbit … the name *Chinook* salmon is capitalized because it is a proper noun, taken from the name of a tribe of Native Americans from the state of Washington.

Link: Alaska Department of Fish and Game
http://www.adfg.state.ak.us/

ADF&G Wildlife Notebook Series
http://www.adfg.state.ak.us/pubs/notebook/notehome.php

Chapter Twenty-Three
Kenai Peninsula

Beautiful scenery is even better when the weather is beautiful, too.

Thursday, September 19, 1996

Hello.

My, what an extraordinary day I have had. Actually, two days were involved but today is the one that I will want to remember. I guess that I must have seen about 50 mountain goats. And about that many glaciers, too. Today, I was on one of the most memorable flights that I will remember, despite the fact that 24 hours ago I would not have believed that the events of today would actually happen and I was praying that they would not.

Here is how the story goes. Early yesterday, I flew on a commercial flight from Anchorage to Homer with 16 other people. Altogether, we were various staff representing the Exxon Valdez Oil Spill Restoration Program, each in our own way and each for a different purpose. We were on a field trip that included community forums to talk with as many local people as we could in each of three places, Homer, Seldovia, and Port Graham. We wanted to give them information about the status of the projects and the program, answer their questions, and listen to their concerns. In addition, most of the group—others, not I—were there to examine several pieces of property that are under consideration for possible purchase by Exxon Valdez Oil Spill Restoration funds.

After we arrived in Homer yesterday, we boarded a chartered tour boat, about 50 feet long, for a trip across Kachemak Bay to Seldovia. It was raining and windy, but the captain was confident that it would be a safe trip. He was a good captain, but things really did go downhill fast from there. Everything seemed all right as we rounded the end of Homer Spit and headed out across the bay. Soon, however, the seas were running about 10 feet tall with some swells even taller and with about a 2 foot chop on top of that.

The boat bucked and lunged off each wave. But the boat churned on.

Of all the travelers, fully half were seriously seasick. Half or more of the remaining travelers were on the edge, too. But the boat churned on. Only three passengers were still standing at the end of the 20-mile trip.

It was not fun.

We had originally planned to go directly to Port Graham to meet with villagers and later transfer to Seldovia for a second meeting, where we would spend the night because there was no place to stay in Port Graham. The wind was from the wrong angle and the water was too rough to reach Port Graham, so we went ashore directly into Seldovia.

Before we could settle in and relax, however, someone came up with the idea of flying to Port Graham for the meeting! I was among the group of four who were selected to go. It was a short, but awful flight. It was big time *bad*! Visibility was horrid and the wind was rocking us all over. The plane was shaking and rolling and the pilot took us down at a steep angle. It was one of the roughest flights I have been on. We finally rolled to a bumpy stop on the gravel runway.

Before the meeting started, we had a good meal of dishes prepared by the Natives—about half the recipes had salmon. One interesting menu item was herring roe on kelp. I tried it but was not impressed.

The meeting was good but we could not see all the things that we had wanted to see because of the pouring rain. We flew back to Seldovia. The weather seemed to be improving. But the rain continued to fall. This trip was a little less harrowing.

We took a break. Then, we had a wonderful supper of grilled salmon and halibut, halibut chowder, wild rice, and wild blueberry cobbler for dessert. We had a good meeting with the villagers after the supper. Afterwards, as we walked back to our lodging, we could pick out a few stars in the partly cloudy sky. Despite the pleasant ending to this day, we were all concerned, apprehensive, and skeptical about the weather because we were scheduled to return across Kachemak Bay to Homer by boat and later we were to fly back to Anchorage.

This morning, however, it was calm. It was mostly clear. Most of the clouds were over the mountains and they slowly coalesced and rose higher off the mountains. The sunrise was very pretty. The seas were calm. There was only a slight swell. The sky was a brilliant blue—the kind of blue that appears only after the cleansing action of a storm. The clouds continued to merge and become better formed.

We boarded the boat and began our passage. The shadowy, ominous gray clouds morphed into a playground of bright whites that were silhouetted before the deep-blue sky. Scattered everywhere across the traverse were big and small clusters of birds and sea mammals. Scoters, murres, murrelets, cormorants, loons, gulls, and sea otters. All were busy feeding and relocating after the several-day storm. It was beautiful. It was just a wonderful, gorgeous boat ride to start our day. Unlike our trip just the day before, not one person became seasick.

Before noon, we drove north of town and hiked down a path to the shore to tour the site of a newly purchased property that will become a state park. We could not see much because it was undeveloped, but it does include some wonderful tide pools.

We visited several potential properties for purchase and another project site. Later, we had a good meeting with the people of Homer.

But then it was time to return to Anchorage.

Our plan was to return on a charter flight so we could look over some special real estate along the way. It was best seen from the air. In fact this special terrain is accessible only by air or by boat. And as it happens, the best aircraft that was available to transport this many people was a special aircraft. We flew in a vintage DC-3. This aircraft had been refitted to recreate a feeling of flying in the 1940s. Nevertheless, even though the weather looked good, I doubt that any of us had expected to complete this trip as planned. *I* certainly did not think that we would complete the trip as planned. Otherwise, the DC-3 was perfect for this trip because it could accommodate all the passengers and with top speeds of 100 to 150 miles per hour, we could have a good look at the landscapes along the way.

Oh my, what a flight! The trip was magnificent! We flew virtually the entire outer length of the Kenai Peninsula. This was on the outside of the peninsula. We flew along the outer coast where it meets the Gulf of Alaska. This coastline had been oiled by the spill but now it was clean.

This was the kind of trip that few people would normally take. And, probably some two-thirds of all the days of any year, it would not be flyable because of bad weather. We saw mountain goats. They were mostly small spots of white on the greenish-grey, seemingly vertical slopes, but some were close. And glaciers. We saw so many glaciers. They were everywhere. They were mostly huge streaks of white with long black streaks of the rocky rubble lateral moraines. Some intertidal inlets were huge, some were small. Lakes and lagoons reflected all shades of blue and green. There were spire-like mountaintops and a 900-foot-tall waterfall.

The sunshine was brilliant in the crystal-clear newly cleansed air. Colors

The outer Kenai Peninsula coast includes spectacular views of islands, waterfalls and glaciers, especially on a clear, calm day.

were intense and multihued: deep greens, azures. Bright blues and brilliant whites. Mountain slopes and vertical cliffs showed dark greens and blacks. Crashing, foaming white waves. The bright sun sparkled like broken glass off the small waves. Tall, vertical, cascading white streaks turned into waterfalls or remnants of snow that filled narrow gullies. There were pastels, too, of the changing season: pinks, oranges, greens, browns. Light gray. Blue. Green.

The clouds became enormous, tall towers and rounded cumulus bulbs. Grayish white below and overtopped with striking white hovering in the dark blue sky.

And the DC-3 droned onward.

It was a wonderful and most memorable flight. Smooth and steady. Spontaneous, breathtaking scenery. Just when I thought I had seen the most impressive view, another appeared. We reached Resurrection Bay and turned inland toward Anchorage.

It did have to end. We flew up over Seward and through a rainbow. Soon we were over Kenai Lake. We looked down and saw the Russian River. And Anchorage at last. It had to end.

This was the flight that had to end. It was at the end of a wonderfully special

Seward, at the head of Resurrection Bay, is pinched in between the bay and the mountain.

day. Yesterday, we did not think that today was possible. But with all the special things, the sights, the sounds and smells, the skies, and the clear air, that so often follow closely after a storm, I suppose that we should not have been surprised. What a wonderful, classic flight in a wonderful, classic aircraft.

Often, a payback is not pleasant. Today, our payback for a day of bad weather just yesterday, was truly extraordinary.

Gotta go. Later.

Bill

February 12, 2009

Oh, wait, there is more ... You have probably heard this before, but airplanes and Alaskans just go along together. It has been awhile since I have seen the old DC-3s in Anchorage and that is quite sad. That was a terrific aircraft for a leisurely flightseeing trip. Karel and I took one trip with a flight plan that began in Anchorage and traveled up the Knik River and Glacier, over the Chugach Mountains, into Prince William Sound, down College Fjord, and returned over Portage Pass and Turnagain Arm. Unfortunately, we were never able to take another flight that circumnavigated Mount McKinley. That would have been a magnificent flight on a clear day such as the one we had when we flew the outer Kenai Peninsula coast. Nevertheless, it is always easy to arrange for a flightseeing trip or an air taxi dropoff and pickup.

Anchorage is the largest community in Alaska and there are air traffic connections worldwide as well as throughout Alaska. The Ted Stevens International Airport in Anchorage began operation as Anchorage International Airport in 1951 and by the 1960s the city became known as the Air Crossroads of the World. Most visitors and most air freight arrive in Alaska through the international airport and, of course, many travelers from bush Alaska also come through this airport. It is entertaining to watch baggage from flights that arrived from instate flights as it rides around the luggage carousel. You will see tool boxes, outboard motors and collapsible boats, coolers, backpacks, moose or caribou antlers with any sort of improvised protectors over the sharp tines, fishing gear, and more.

It seems that small aircraft are everywhere in Alaska. A dozen or so neighborhood airstrips are sprinkled around Anchorage subdivisions and there is an airstrip in most communities throughout Alaska. Some people even have private airstrips. Of course, floatplanes also abound. Many lakes in Anchorage have slips for privately owned floatplanes. Most villages are served by an airstrip, many of which are unpaved. There are, in fact, more pilots per capita in Alaska than in any other state in the nation.

Adjacent to the Ted Stevens International Airport is the Lake Hood Air Harbor, the busiest floatplane base in the world. Lake Hood is connected to Lake Spenard by a long dredged channel that serves as a taxiway. There are also additional dredged channels with slips and tiedowns. But this is not enough. Some floatplanes are also equipped with wheels on the floats and are semi-amphibious. Some floatplanes slide up on dollies so they can be pulled out of the water and parked in floatplane parking lots. True amphibian aircraft like the Grumman Goose are strange at first to ride in. You take off from a runway like any other wheeled aircraft but when the Goose lands on a water body, the belly is underwater and the spray is at eye level. During winter, many floatplanes are changed out and equipped with skis.

Of course, small, wheeled aircraft can use the runways, but most of the small wheeled aircraft are across town at Merrill Field, which was established in 1930. Merrill Field was the only airport in Anchorage until the international airport began operations. Today, it is a public-use, general aviation airport and it is one of the busiest in the nation. Merrill Field is owned by the City of Anchorage and it houses about a thousand aircraft.

The original airfield in Anchorage was just a few blocks south of present-day downtown Anchorage. That airstrip was developed into our Delaney Park Strip, roughly a city block wide and 11 blocks long. Today, this grassy park is used for tennis, baseball, basketball, kite flyers, special events like the annual Governor's Picnic, and more.

Helicopters are also available in many parts of the state. Over the years they have become ubiquitous and they have become an invaluable asset for working, search and rescue, and medical emergencies.

You may wonder why there are so many airplanes in Alaska. Alaska is a big land with lots of space and few roads. Airplanes, big and small, are important for commerce, work, and recreation.

One last tidbit. The de Havilland DHC-2 Beaver was developed in Canada in 1947. It is popular throughout Alaska as a dependable workhorse to haul big loads in remote locations. It can operate on wheels, floats, and skis. Although production was ended in 1967, many are still operating in Alaska.

Link: Visit the Alaska Aviation Heritage Museum
http://www.alaskaairmuseum.org/

Chapter Twenty-Four
Paint River

The best laid plans are always weather dependent in Alaska.

Saturday, June 5, 1982

Hello.

Well, I just got back from checking our tent. The other tent. Again. It hasn't blown away yet. Boy, I'd sure be happy if the wind would die down. I'd judge that it's blowing about 25 miles per hour and gusting to 40. At least, it was down some 10 to 15 miles per hour from about noon when we went out to swing that tent around so it would face the wind better. We reinforced all the stakes and double-guyed the corners.

Alan, Rick, and I use that tent for sleeping and storing our personal gear. The tent we are in now is a 10-by-12-foot wall tent supported by a framework of 2-by-4s. This tent is for storing our equipment, cooking, and eating. If the other one goes down, we can sleep here, too. I think everything will be okay, though, because the angle of the wind keeps shifting slowly and, we think, the wind is very slowly dying.

Our camp at the mouth of the Paint River was snug but adequate. One tent was for sleeping, the other was for cooking and other general use. (ADF&G Photo)

Right now, we don't have much work to do so I thought I'd write to you. I've already finished the Louis L'Amour book I brought. I'm sure who I should direct this letter to. I owe many people letters. If you won't mind too much, I'll just write one long letter which I can copy and share with several people. I'll try to write more, too, to each of you. I expect I'll have plenty of time, in fact, more time than I care to imagine, if we cannot get out of here tomorrow.

Where to start? Ah, where indeed? I am at the mouth of the Paint River. If you look on a map, the Paint River is on the west side of Cook Inlet, across from Homer. Southwest from Augustine Island, an active volcano. The Paint River is one drainage north of the McNeil River which is famous for its midsummer concentration of brown bears. Oh, and we are southeast of Lake Iliamna, too.

Why? We are here to evaluate whether the installation of a fish pass at the mouth of the Paint River may be useful to allow spawning salmon to enter the river. The river has about 25 to 30 miles of good-quality spawning gravel, but the river also has a 40-foot high vertical waterfall right at the height of tide. It's a big river. I estimate about 1,500 cubic feet per second.

When? I came to Homer last Friday, a week ago, so we could fly over here to land on the beach at high tide on Saturday. It was a 90-mile, hourlong flight. Unfortunately, there was a fog bank along this shore so we were delayed until Sunday. Fortunately, the king salmon season opened on Friday night at midnight. Unfortunately, this has been a very late spring in this part of Alaska so few fish were in the river. Nick took me to the Anchor River where I had one hooked for a moment or two and I helped him land a small one, perhaps 25 pounds.

Anyhow, the float planes landed here on the high tide at about 9 p.m. last Sunday night. By about midnight, we had most of our camp and gear moved off the beach and up the *steep* 50- to 60- foot bluff. Our sleeping tent was set up, some supper was eaten, and we were ready for bed.

What else? The next two days each began about 6 a.m. and ended about 10 p.m. Fortunately, it's light now from about 3 a.m. until 11 p.m. On a clear night, it is not really dark. Last week, at midnight on the Anchor River, I needed to use my flashlight only once or twice.

We had to set up this wall tent. Then we had to run a line across the river at the mouth of the narrow canyon, about a quarter mile below the falls. To this, we attached a trap and the holding box to recapture experimentally released fish. Before that, we sewed the net onto the net frame and repaired the holding box, which a bear had damaged after Alan had cached it in anticipation of this work trip. It also took a bit of time for Rick to pump up our inflatable rubber raft, which has a 15-horsepower outboard engine. We selected and marked out a landing area for the helicopter to lower a fish tank to deliver some pink salmon fry that had been scheduled for the test on Monday afternoon. We barely managed to install another fish trap with an 18-foot wing just before the fry were delivered and were released about 6 miles upstream

The boat is inflated and ready for work and the fry recapture net is assembled on the frame. Floats will be attached and it will be floated to the sampling site. (ADF&G Photo)

The Paint River ends with a 50-foot, vertical waterfall at the head of tide. (ADF&G Photo)

Our arrival had been delayed a day. Unfortunately, the fish delivery was not. We had to bust butt to have everything ready for the test.

But it was worth the effort. Believe me; I was ecstatic when we started catching some fry within minutes after getting the upstream trap fishing! Some fry made the 6-mile trip from the release site within 1½ hours! Most arrived in about 4 hours. In addition to the fry release, we performed several other experiments. In one, we released a number of floats to determine the rate of passing the falls and the behavior of the currents. We learned that it took as little as 4 minutes to travel over the falls and into our downstream trap, a distance of about a quarter mile. Some of the floats, and some fry, too, no doubt, spent an hour or more caught in an eddy.

Why? The Alaska Department of Fish and Game is developing a plan to install a fish ladder to allow spawning salmon to get over the falls but we also needed to know if migrating fry would survive a trip over the falls if a spawning population was established. We determined that the fry can physically survive the falls but we are still concerned that they may not survive the problem of potential gas supersaturation, a problem much like diver's bends—because of the very deep plunge pool at the base of the falls. In addition, there may not be enough plankton in the small estuary to support all the fry which may be produced by this large system, so we took the boat out the day before yesterday to sample plankton.

A helicopter brought a load of pink salmon fry from a Tutka Hatchery near Homer. The fry were released above the falls and a sample was recaptured to determine if they could survive the passage over the falls. (ADF&G Photo)

Other? Fortunately, we have finally been able to relax. After we had our camp and our gear set up, the fish delivered, and our experiments finished in two days instead of the three we had scheduled. Everything in Alaska is weather dependent.

We did some beachcombing. We walked 2 or 3 miles of beach searching mainly for glass Japanese fishing floats. We looked quite hard and I was very lucky to find one. It was quite ordinary, but I was pleased to find it. We found net floats and flotsam of about every description. Then we found a clam bed. A very big clam bed! With our bare hands, we gathered more clams than even we could eat!

Just being here is an adventure for me. On the day we flew in, someone saw a grizzly, or brown bear from the plane shortly before we landed. We saw one from our camp on the second day and, while we were in the boat making a plankton tow, we saw two more about 4 miles down the beach. Fortunately, none have been too close or in our camp yet. Nevertheless, we keep our short barrel 12 gauge shotgun handy, especially at night. It is loaded with slugs and 000 buckshot. Alan found a large skull from an old bear on the beach and most of the beaches have bear tracks. I can barely cover some of the tracks with my cap. The imprint of the pads of most tracks is about the size of my hand.

Newly free-swimming pink salmon fry are about an inch long. The fry used in the test run have been fed and are slightly longer. (ADF&G Photo)

We saw a wolverine and two foxes. It was a special treat to see the wolverine. They are rarely seen. We saw one fox while we were out in our boat. As we watched, it came around the edge of a cliff and we drifted closer. It didn't mind us at all, but went directly to a gull's nest and grabbed an egg. It headed back around the cliff, to its den and young, no doubt. It only dropped the egg once as the gulls screamed and dive-bombed him!

Birds are abundant. Lots of gulls, harlequin ducks, two or three eagles, shorebirds, guillemots, some puffins.

Largely, it has been a great trip! Now, if only the wind would lie down a bit. Whoa. Suppertime!

We keep eating big meals even though we're not as active as we were at first. Not much else to do today besides checking the tent occasionally. Later, we will need to go down to the beach to move the boat higher. We need to keep it above the 18-foot tide that is predicted for about one a.m. We went to the beach briefly earlier today. At the top of the bluff, Rick faced into the wind, opened up his coat, and jumped up into the air. He was blown back by the wind 3 feet before he landed. Once while we were working on the tent, it rained briefly. It felt like blown sand grains. Fortunately, we have had nearly no rain.

Actually, we have had two days of beautiful weather and some windy days, too, but nothing like today. When it was sunny and calm, it was really gorgeous. It was great to be here and it's been great to be here on this project.

I rarely get to do this kind of work anymore and I don't spend much time in the field. I'm sure Karel is glad for that! By now, I expect she's a bit haggard. The kids can get to her at times. I guess that is why parents come in twos. I'm glad she's not here right now, but I wish I could share more of this kind of trip with her. She really does enjoy getting out. In about a week, I will need to spend about four days again in the field, but I plan to take Karel and the kids with me, camping, while I work. We can drive to that spot.

But in late July, we have a U.S. Forest Service Cabin reserved on Prince William Sound. I am really looking forward to that trip! We'll fly in for three or four days. With luck, we'll not be weathered in, as we are just now.

I'm sure glad we have this extra tent. It would be absolutely horrid now if we had only the other one. We have the bottom edges all chinked with pieces of muskeg and we have a kerosene heater going, which we share and sort of huddle around.

We have a scheduled radio check with the Homer office at 11 a.m. tomorrow. We all expect, and hope, that the plane can fly and we will be able to get out tomorrow. I'm anxious to see Karel and the kids again. If we don't make it, well, we still have enough food for a week. And we can always go dig more clams, too.

Rick has been washing dishes and he did us a favor. He let Alan and me wash our hands in the warm, soapy water before he tossed it out. Ah, the small pleasures of life!

I do think the wind is starting to lie down a bit.

June 6.

Guess what? It's still blowing. And raining. It started raining about 10 p.m. last night. We'll not be getting out today. Sure hope this breaks soon and we'll get out tomorrow. Our sleeping tent is quite dry—except where something bulges against the side. This tent isn't too bad, but both are noisy. Rick has already finished my Louis L'Amour western paperback. Alan is the lucky one. He still has half of *Chesapeake* to finish. Fortunately, someone who came over on the helicopter with the pink salmon fry sent in some magazines, a newspaper, and refreshments. Unfortunately, we're down to our last beer. At least, I could enjoy the morning paper today. Unfortunately, it is last Saturday's morning paper. And this is the third time I've read it.

Actually, I failed to say that our work tasks are all done and I was scheduled to leave yesterday. Another biologist was supposed to come in by helicopter to run a quick test for gas supersaturation on the fry that were recaptured below the falls. The helicopter could not fly so he didn't make it. Obviously, neither did I. Alan and Rick had been scheduled to leave today.

June 9.

Hey! Hey! We made it out! I was home Monday night about 8:30 p.m. It rained hard on Sunday, but Monday morning it was still but with fog and clouds. We were apprehensive about the weather and getting out, but finally, by noon, the pilot decided it was okay to fly.

While we were waiting for our pickup, we saw that wolverine again, not more than 200 yards from camp. And another red fox. But no bears. We tried hard to see one. We all wanted to see another one, just not close. Oh! I forgot. While we were waiting in Homer before we could get out to here, I saw a cow moose with twin calves chased by a black bear through the backyards and between some houses.

Anyhow this was a great trip and I'm glad I could go. I'm glad to be back, too. Now, maybe things will settle down so I can go fishing!

Bye for now.

Bill

February 18, 2009

Oh, wait, there is more … Pink salmon are both the smallest and the most abundant of the five species of North American Pacific salmon and their life history is different from the other four species because they follow a simple, obligatory two-year life cycle. Of the Pacific salmon, only pink salmon have an entirely predictable life history. Eggs spawned in one year hatch as fry the following spring, migrate to the ocean, where they spend just over a year growing and maturing so they can return to spawn in the second year and restart the cycle. Most pink salmon populations exhibit an odd- and even-year pattern of abundance over much of their range, which extends around the North Pacific Ocean from central California to Japan and Russia.

Pink salmon are anadromous, like all salmon. They spawn in freshwater and migrate to the ocean to feed and grow. Pink salmon spawn in the lower reaches of streams and rivers. In fact, many populations spawn in the upper intertidal reaches and in the adjacent upstream reaches. In southcentral Alaska, spawning is in August. Eggs are fertilized by the males and buried in nest-like redds by the females. Females spend eight or more days on the redd before spawning is complete. After spawning, the salmon die.

Eggs incubate and larvae develop and hatch as alevins in midwinter. The alevins reside in the redd while they use up nutrients from the yolk sac and emerge from the gravel in April and May.

The slender, inch-long, silvery fry migrate immediately to salt water. Neither pink nor chum salmon have a juvenile freshwater residence, but the other salmon do. After the young pink salmon fry enter salt water, they travel along the shorelines in large, dense schools as they begin to feed on small planktonic organisms. Survival from the time of egg deposit to this early feeding stage rarely exceeds 20 per cent.

As the young fish grow, they can eat larger food, including fish, squid, and invertebrates, to grow faster and bigger. Bigger fish swim faster, survive better and larger-sized females produce more and larger eggs which, in turn, survive better. Average survival of pink salmon from fry to returning adult is usually about 2 to 3 per cent.

While in the ocean, pink salmon maintain loose schools that migrate around the Gulf of Alaska and the North Pacific Ocean. They swim mostly within the upper 50 feet of the water column. During their oceanic migrations, it is believed that salmon can utilize a navigation system based on the sun angle or the earth's electromagnetic field. As they return closer to shore they have more cues to use and in the estuary and freshwater, salmon use an odor memory of the stream that was imprinted in their brain as young fry to return to their home stream.

The average size of mature pink salmon is around 4 pounds. The largest pink salmon reported from Alaska waters is 8 pounds; however, I have heard a report of a 15.4-pound pink salmon from the lower Stillaguamish River north of Seattle.

Pink salmon are mostly harvested by commercial fishermen with purse seines and most of the harvest is processed for a canned product. Some operators, however, process pink salmon for specialty markets, including frozen, boneless, skinless fillets, and fish patties. The flesh is usually a pale pink. Unfortunately, like all salmon, pink salmon stop feeding when they enter freshwater and the flesh quality deteriorates as spawning progresses. Consequently, pink salmon caught in freshwater are often not highly regarded as table fare.

The 2008 commercial harvest of pink salmon in Alaska was 84,051,000 fish, nearly 60 per cent of the total number of salmon harvested. These were sold by the fishermen for a total of $86,243,000, just over 20 per cent of the total 2008 salmon commercial catch value to the fishermen of $409,324,000.

The total estimated statewide pink salmon sport fish harvest of pink salmon in 2007 was 754,767 fish.

Pink salmon also have an alias. They are known as humpback salmon or, simply, humpy. Undoubtedly, this refers to the distinct, tall hump that forms on the back of the male pink salmon during spawning. This is not unique to pink salmon, but it is more pronounced for pink salmon than other salmon. One can speculate that the purpose of the hump is twofold. It may make them more attractive to females and it may make them appear more intimidating to other males as they defend the redd and the spawning female.

One last tidbit. It is said that there are exceptions to every rule. Exceptions to the rule of the pink salmon's two-year life cycle are rare. Only a few examples of one-year-old or three-year-old mature pink salmon have been found in wild populations, but one-, two-, and three-year-old mature pink salmon are found in the Great Lakes from a single release of a transplanted stock.

Link: Alaska Department of Fish and
Game Wildlife Notebook series, Pink Salmon
http://www.adfg.state.ak.us/pubs/notebook/fish/pink.php

End Note

June 6, 2009.

Hello again.

Thank you for letting me share these stories about Alaska with you. This project has allowed me to relive some of my experiences, revisit the places, and remember the people who were there with me. Karel and I still live in Anchorage and we still love to visit Alaska as often as we can.

I hope you have enjoyed these experiences with me and learned about some new places to visit and a little of what life is like in Alaska.

For now, goodbye. I'll talk with you later, okay?

Bill